LEADER'S GUIDE

10 LESSONS ON THE HOLY SPIRIT

JOHN SIMS

Unless otherwise indicated, Scripture quotations are taken from the *Holy Bible, New International Version*® NIV®. Copyright © 1973, 1978, 1984 by International Bible Society. Used by permission of Zondervan Publishing House. All rights reserved.

Scripture quotations marked NKJV are taken from the *New King James Version*. Copyright © 1979, 1980, 1982, 1990, 1995, Thomas Nelson Inc., Publishers.

Scripture quotations marked KJV are from the King James Version of the Bible.

Scripture quotations marked RSV are taken from the *Revised Standard Version* of the Bible. Copyright © 1946, 1952, 1971 by the Division of Christian Education of the National Council of the Churches of Christ in the USA. Used by permission.

Scripture quotations marked NLT are taken from the *Holy Bible, New Living Translation*, copyright © 1996. Used by permission of Tyndale House Publishers, Inc., Wheaton, Illinois 60189. All rights reserved.

Scripture quotations marked NASB are taken from the *New American Standard Bible*®. Copyright © The Lockman Foundation 1960, 1962, 1963, 1968, 1971, 1972, 1973, 1975, 1977, 1995. Used by permission.

Managing Editor: Lance Colkmire
Editorial Assistant: Tammy Hatfield
Copy Editor: Esther Metaxas
Technical Design: Tammy Henkel
Cover Design: Michael McDonald

ISBN: 978-1-59684-689-0

Copyright © 2012 by Pathway Press
1080 Montgomery Avenue
Cleveland, TN 37311

All rights reserved. No part of this publication may be reproduced or transmitted in any form or by any means, electronic or mechanical, including photocopying, recording, or otherwise, or by any information storage or retrieval system, without the permission in writing from the publisher. Please direct inquiries to Pathway Press, 1080 Montgomery Avenue, Cleveland, TN 37311.

Visit *www.pathwaypress.org* for more information.

Printed in the United States of America

DEDICATION

This work is affectionately dedicated to our grandchildren in the trust that the ministry of the Holy Spirit will be as real in their lives as He has in ours:
Mary,
Megan,
David,
Noah,
Isaac,
and to the memory of our first grandson,
Christopher Mark.

Table of Contents

Preface 8

Introduction 9

Lesson 1   The Spirit of Truth 11

Lesson 2   The Person of the Holy Spirit 19

Lesson 3   The Holy Spirit in the Old Testament 29

Lesson 4   The Holy Spirit in the Life and Ministry of Jesus 39

Lesson 5   Living in the Spirit 47

Lesson 6   Spiritual Gifting in the Church 57

Lesson 7   Baptism in the Holy Spirit 65

Lesson 8   The Holy Spirit and Eschatology 77

Lesson 9   The Pentecostal Century 89

Lesson 10 Our Pentecostal Identity 107

PREFACE

Over a century has passed since the latter rain began to fall at Azusa Street. Since that time, the Pentecostal message and experience has spread around the world. But no religious movement is more than one generation removed from extinction. The purpose of this study is to ignite fresh interest in the person and work of the Holy Spirit and to encourage a new hunger for the power and purpose of Pentecost. This study is offered in the hope that it will help kindle a greater appreciation for the movement and its commitments.

The need for divine guidance is never more deeply felt than when one undertakes to teach about the Holy Spirit. All who study these lessons are encouraged to do so with an open Bible and a prayerful heart. This material is presented from a classical Pentecostal perspective and bears witness to a faith and an experience that is true to Scripture and relevant to the needs of the church today. It is organized around key doctrines and issues as well as a historical perspective from which classical Pentecostal theology can be identified and articulated.

The making of a book is a task that involves many people. There are those who inspire it, those who encourage and stand by the author during the writing process, and those who actually put the book together. I would like to thank all of those who fit into one or more of these categories. As always, Pat, my wife and best friend, has been my inspiration and encourager. Special acknowledgment is due all those at Pathway Press who played a vital role in preparing this study for publication, especially Lance Colkmire and Dan Black. Special love and gratitude is extended to all who taught and nurtured me in the faith.

INTRODUCTION

Since the turn of the twentieth century, the signs of the Holy Spirit have been everywhere. The great resurgence of the Holy Spirit that has swept the church has created a hunger for a deeper understanding and experience of God, spawning a renewal movement that has revitalized the doctrine and worship of the church. The Spirit does not belong to any particular tradition; He blows where He will. The Holy Spirit indwells believers and contextualizes His presence and power in diverse traditions and cultural settings, but we know that the norm and pattern of the Spirit's ministry is the inspired Word of God.

No one should think that he or she has all the answers regarding the person and work of the Holy Spirit, but it is instructive to remember that Jesus said the Holy Spirit is the Spirit of Truth. It is the nature of the Spirit to teach those who have open hearts and minds about Himself. The lessons in this study on the Holy Spirit are biblically based. They can be used by church groups (e.g., in midweek or Sunday school settings), by student and neighborhood groups, or for individual study in the home.

The lessons are designed for 45-60 minute sessions, unless the group chooses to take more time. This study on the Holy Spirit can fit well into a quarterly system in the local church, or a semester system in a college or Bible school. If studied in a group setting, there should be a discussion leader who will thoroughly prepare before the group meets and facilitate group discussion. All participants should study the lesson summaries carefully and familiarize themselves with the biblical texts provided for each lesson. A glossary of key terms and concepts used in each lesson is provided in the lesson material.

A standard translation of the Bible should be used. A paraphrase edition is not recommended. A video introduction to each lesson is provided. Use your smartphone to access the video via the QR codes.

These lessons are meant to be personally applied. They are offered in the hope that this study will be a life-transforming experience for you. As you begin each lesson, pray that the Holy Spirit will help you understand and apply the truth of that lesson to your life.

Lesson 1

The Spirit of Truth

Jesus taught His disciples that the Holy Spirit is the Spirit of Truth (John 14:17). In this first lesson, we will discuss the ministry of the Holy Spirit in relation to the great truths that God has revealed through the inspired Word of God. The Scriptures are authoritative for Christians in all matters relating to belief and practice. It is therefore imperative that we understand the basis of that authority. This will require us to focus on the work of the Spirit in relation to (1) the inspiration of Scripture, (2) the inner witness of the Holy Spirit to the truth of Scripture, and (3) the illumination of Scripture.

As the Spirit of Truth, the Holy Spirit worked through human authors to bring us the inspired written Word (the Bible). His work in relation to the Word, however, is an ongoing work, as the Spirit of Truth helps the believer better understand, interpret, and obey the Scriptures. The internal witness of the Spirit is vital to the believer's assurance and confidence in the truth of the Bible.

I. THE INSPIRATION OF SCRIPTURE
(John 16:13-15; 2 Peter 1:21; 2 Tim. 3:16-17; John 10:35)

A. *Inspiration*, with regard to the Bible, refers to the work of the Holy Spirit that enabled the human authors to record what God willed to be written in the Scriptures. This inspiration extends to both the Old and New Testaments. Our English word *inspiration* comes from the Greek word *theopneustos* that means "God-breathed," referring to the creative, life-giving activity of the Holy Spirit in bringing to us the Word of God. Jesus told His disciples that after His departure the Holy Spirit would glorify Him and lead them into truth concerning Himself (see John 16:14).

It is the purpose of the Holy Spirit to reveal Christ to us and extend the kingdom of God that Christ proclaimed. The truth the Holy Spirit brings to us is Christ-centered truth. Through the ministry of the Spirit, the apostles were enabled to understand and record for us a true understanding of the redemptive work of Jesus Christ.

Jesus promised them in His parting discourse, "He will guide you into all truth" (v. 13). The truth Jesus was referring to was not truth concerning the Spirit but concerning Himself. It would be the will of the Holy Spirit to reveal Himself in the face of Christ.

B. The exact manner used by the Holy Spirit to bring us the inspired Word of God is a mystery we do not fully understand, but we do know the Spirit worked through the personalities, style, experiences, and cultural/historical context of those who wrote the Bible. They were not dictated to or controlled by the Spirit in any manner that excluded the human factor. All the while, the Spirit was divinely guiding and superintending the process so the outcome would be the Word of God. This is typical of the ministry of the Holy Spirit who wills to guide and direct us, but never in a forceful or controlling manner. The apostle Peter describes it this way: "Holy men of God spoke as they were moved by the Holy Spirit" (2 Peter 1:21 NKJV).

The extent of the Spirit's influence was to the very words of Scripture (*verbal inspiration*) and throughout the whole of the Old and New Testaments (*plenary inspiration*). Paul assured young Timothy that the God-breathed Scriptures are "useful for teaching, rebuking, correcting and training in righteousness, so that the man of God may be thoroughly equipped for every good work" (2 Tim. 3:16-17).

Because the Scriptures are divinely inspired, they are trustworthy; and because they are trustworthy, they are our source of *authority* for what we believe and practice. Many today want to live independent of any authority for their life. It is a word many reject, but the fact is we live by authority every day. We cannot live without it; the issue is, which authority we will live by. An authority is simply something or someone we deem trustworthy. In this sense, our lives are filled with authorities. We trust our physician and take the medicine she prescribes because we trust her expertise and medical experience. We board a plane and place our life in the hands of a pilot to fly us safely from one continent to another because we trust that the pilot is highly trained and experienced. In a similar manner, we entrust our lives and our future to the God of Scripture because we believe the Bible is more than a human document. It is the very Word of God, inspired by the Holy Spirit, that we can fully trust.

Many literary and artistic works are inspired in the sense that they are the products of human creativity and genius—for example, the works of Shakespeare and the music of Beethoven. The Word of God, on the other hand, has been uniquely and creatively breathed upon (i.e., given truth and life) from above.

II. THE INNER WITNESS OF THE HOLY SPIRIT
(John 14:26; 15:26; 16:13)

A. God uses human reason in many ways, but our trust in the Bible is more than a claim that makes intellectual sense. The internal coherence of the Bible, its unity, and its consistency with the facts of history, archeology, and human experience all witness to its trustworthiness. But God has not left the integrity of His Word to human reason alone. The Holy Spirit is God's faithful witness to the truth of Christ and the Scriptures. The *inner testimony of the Spirit* gives assurance and certainty regarding the truth of Scripture. Human reason operating without the aid of the Holy Spirit easily breeds doubt and uncertainty, but the Spirit breathes certainty.

The Holy Spirit is not a skeptic. In uncertain times like our own, where skepticism and doubt abound regarding the truth of Christ and the Scriptures, we must have the inner witness of the Spirit. Doubt can never be fully dealt with in the human heart and mind apart from the witness of the Holy Spirit. Divine things must have divine certainty, a persuasion that can only come from God. The same Spirit that spoke through the prophets and apostles must penetrate our heart and mind if we are to be fully persuaded of God's truth. This is why Jesus told His disciples the Holy Spirit would bear witness to Him (John 14:26; 15:26; 16:13).

B. It is important to emphasize that the truth inwardly witnessed to by the Holy Spirit is not a mere feeling or opinion to be contrasted with real knowledge. It is a true knowledge of God's will and purpose toward us that culminates in the work of Jesus Christ. It is, as John Calvin described, "a firm and certain knowledge of God's benevolence toward us, founded upon the truth of the freely given promise in Christ, both revealed to our minds and sealed upon our hearts by the Holy Spirit" (*Institutes of the Christian Religion*, Book III, ch. II, sec. Vii).

It is the ministry of the Holy Spirit to take the things of Christ and make them real to us. Without the Spirit, the Word is a mere letter, law, writing. He turns the written Word into the living Word, giving assurance and joy to what we hear and see from Scripture. It must be remembered, however, that His witness is always given within the context of the Bible. In our preaching and teaching, the *unity of Word and Spirit* must always be maintained.

III. THE ILLUMINATION OF SCRIPTURE
(Ps. 119:18; 1 Cor. 2:12-16; Matt. 13:11, 16; John 14:24; 15:26; 16:13-14, 24)

A. The inspiration of Scripture refers to the work of the Holy Spirit in enabling the human authors of the Bible to record what God willed to give in the Scriptures. The illumination of Scripture by the Holy Spirit refers to the work of the Spirit that assists believers in understanding, interpreting, and obeying the Scriptures. The Spirit works to nurture our understanding so that we can grow more deeply into the Word of God.

The psalmist was asking for *illumination* when he prayed, "Open thou mine eyes, that I may behold wondrous things out of thy law" (Ps. 119:18 KJV). Paul told the Corinthians that believers had received the Spirit, "that we might know the things that are freely given to us of God" (1 Cor. 2:12 KJV). Spiritual things, he said, are spiritually discerned. The Holy Spirit desires that we experience an ongoing growth into the meaning of Scripture and a strengthening of our will to obey what we have come to understand. As we grow more deeply into the Word, we will grow more deeply into Christ.

B. The Spirit's work of illumination allows the believer to experience a holy relevance with regard to the Bible. We are not living in the third, the eleventh, or the nineteenth century. We are living in the twenty-first, and it is realistic to admit that we face new conditions and problems. The old truths are still valid, but sometimes there is a need for new applications. The believer always stands in need of the guidance and understanding the Holy Spirit can give to the changing conditions of life.

Growing into the truth of Scripture does not mean that believers are free to establish new meanings and foundations for their faith. Changing "thought patterns" and "behavior" in society never justify the abandonment of Bible truth. The Holy Spirit will never lead anyone into a non-Christian religion or into a spirituality that is not centered in the Word of God. There are no "new revelations" that have Christian significance outside the Bible. The illuminating work of the Spirit provides the believer with deepening insight and more complete submission to biblical truth and its widening application to human life and need.

The illuminating work of the Holy Spirit is not an arbitrary act of the Spirit but a conditional work based on the condition of our heart and mind. It is for those who have childlike humility, are sincere, and prayerfully desire to know the truth of God. The Spirit of Truth always stands ready to assist those who have a meek and humble spirit. Jesus said that some things were hidden from the wise and prudent but revealed to babes (see Matt. 11:25).

C. The illuminating ministry of the Holy Spirit that takes place in the life of individuals can occur as well in religious communities and movements. When it does, the Holy Spirit often brings out of this illumination something historically significant that enlightens the church concerning a special dimension of God's truth and purpose.

Several examples come to mind. In the sixteenth century, the Holy Spirit led the Protestant Reformers into a fuller understanding of the authority of Scripture, justification by grace alone through faith, the priesthood of believers, and other scriptural doctrines. During the eighteenth century, the Holy Spirit led John Wesley and others into a fuller insight of sanctification and holiness. It was a special time in history that greatly influenced life in England and America. At the turn of the twentieth century, there was a sovereign move of God around the world that manifested itself in gifts of the Holy Spirit and charismatic activity. It shook the Christian world and led to a great movement of spiritual renewal. The church's understanding of the work and ministry of the Holy Spirit was broadened, and a great hunger ensued for a deeper relationship with God. In these, and other historical examples too numerous to mention, the church grew more deeply into the truth of the Word of God. What was already complete in the Word became more completely understood and sought for through the illumination of the Holy Spirit.

LIFE APPLICATION

The life story of John Wesley (1703-1791) is a graphic example of our need for the assurance that can only come from the inner witness of the Holy Spirit. Young Wesley struggled with questions and doubts

God With *Us and* In *Us*

as a divinity student at Oxford and as an Anglican priest. How could he know for sure that he was really a converted man? Which of the Christian traditions, if any, had the truth? These, and other questions, played havoc with the mind of Wesley. Before his father Samuel's death, he had spoken to John about the inner witness of the Spirit, but John had not experienced the assurance his father spoke about. As a minister who was supposed to be sure of his salvation, John Wesley was living a miserable life of uncertainty.

When Wesley traveled to America on a mission to convert the Indians, he experienced further doubts. His mission was a failure. On his return trip, during a ferocious storm at sea, his doubts and questions persisted. He felt that he could no longer live and minister as a priest in a state of such uncertainty. During his trip back to England, Wesley was spiritually challenged. A Moravian pietist named Augustus Spangenberg asked: "Have you the witness within yourself? Does the Spirit of God bear witness with your spirit that you are a child of God?"

Back in London, on May 24, 1738, John Wesley had an experience with God that changed his life. It was his famous "Aldersgate experience," when the Spirit of God moved upon his spirit, sealing the fact of his conversion and assuring him of the truth of the Word of God. In his journal, Wesley described what happened: "In the evening, I went unwillingly to a society meeting on Aldersgate Street where one was reading Luther's *Preface to the Epistle to the Romans*. About a quarter before nine, while he was describing the change God works in the heart through faith in Christ, I felt my heart strangely warmed. I felt I did trust in Christ, Christ alone for my salvation; and an assurance was given me that He had taken away my sins, even mine, and saved me from the law of sin and death."

Wesley later described what had happened to him in biblical terms: "The Spirit itself bore witness to my spirit that I was a child of God" (see Rom. 8:14-17; Gal. 4:4-6). He knew the experience to be real; he had read about it in the New Testament. The unity of Word and Spirit had been wondrously at work in Wesley's life.

What about you? Are the truths of the Bible real in your life? Has the Holy Spirit sealed them in your heart and mind, or do you constantly struggle with doubt and uncertainty? If so, ask the Holy Spirit to make the truth of Scripture real to you and give you the inner assurance and certainty you need to live a victorious Christian life.

DISCUSSSION

The Inspiration of Scripture
1. Describe in your own words what the "inspiration of Scripture" means.
2. What was the role of the Holy Spirit in the inspiration process? What was the human role?
3. Explain why the Scriptures are trustworthy and why they must guide the believer in all matters relating to belief and practice.

The Inner Witness of the Holy Spirit
1. What does the "inner witness of the Holy Spirit" mean? Why is it so important to the believer?
2. Is the internal witness of the Spirit a matter of subjective opinion, or is it true knowledge? Explain your answer.

The Illumination of Scripture
1. Explain what the "illumination of Scripture" means.
2. How important is it for the believer to grow more deeply into the Word of God and be strengthened in will to obey the Word? Share any experience of your own in this regard.

GLOSSARY OF TERMS/CONCEPTS

Authority of Scripture: The Scriptures are authoritative because they are trustworthy (inspired of God). Consequently, they are authoritative for the Christian believer in all matters regarding belief and practice.

Illumination: The ongoing work of the Holy Spirit in the believer and the Christian community that assists them in understanding, interpreting, and growing into a fuller meaning of Scripture. The purpose of this illumination is not for understanding alone but so the believer may more fully trust and obey the revealed truth of God.

Inner Witness of the Holy Spirit: The working of the Holy Spirit in the heart and mind of the believer so as to create confidence and assurance that the Scriptures are true, particularly the promises regarding salvation through faith in Christ.

Inspiration of Scripture: The work of the Holy Spirit that enabled the human authors of the Bible to record what God willed to be written in the Scriptures.

Plenary Inspiration: The view that the superintending work of the Holy Spirit extended to the entire Bible and all its parts.

Unity of Word and Spirit: The Word and the Spirit work together as a single testimony to the truth of God, but in two manifestations: externally through the written Word of Scripture, and internally through the witness and assurance of the Holy Spirit.

Verbal Inspiration: The view that the inspiration of Scripture extends to the words used by the human authors of the Bible.

RESOURCES FOR ADDITIONAL STUDY

Arrington, French L. *Christian Doctrine: A Pentecostal Perspective*. Vol. 1. Cleveland, Tenn.: Pathway, 1992.

Bloesch, Donald G. *Holy Scripture: Revelation*. Downers Grove, Ill.: InterVarsity, 1994.

Horton, Stanley. *What the Bible Says About the Holy Spirit*. Springfield, Mo.: Gospel Publishing, 1976.

Marshall, I. Howard. *Biblical Inspiration*. Grand Rapids: Eerdmans, 1983.

Packer, J. I. *God Has Spoken*, Grand Rapids: Baker, 1994.

Lesson 2

The Person of the Holy Spirit

At the center of the Christian faith is the profound mystery of the Trinity. The mystery is great, but if divine revelation sheds light on it, we should by all means seek to understand what can be known about the triune God. At the heart of this great truth about God is that in His oneness there are three distinctions—Father, Son, and Holy Spirit. This is not a truth that can be grasped by human mathematics, but one that must be understood in the light of divine revelation. As one theologian put it, "Scripture bears witness to a God who demands to be understood in a Trinitarian manner." It is in the context of the great truth of the Trinity that we can begin to grasp something of the person and work of the Holy Spirit.

In this lesson we will have three emphases: (l) the progressive nature of God's self-disclosure in the Old and New Testaments; (2) the relationship of the Holy Spirit to the Father and Son in the inner Trinitarian life of God; and (3) the truth that the outworking of God's plan for creation, redemption, and the nature of His church flows out of the inner life of the Trinity.

From the doctrine of the Trinity we know God exists in a loving relationship of Father, Son, and Holy Spirit, for "God is love" (1 John 4:8). Out of the inner life of the Trinity flows God's loving work of creation, redemption, and the life of the church. The Holy Spirit is more than a mere influence or power; the Spirit is the bond of love between the Father and Son. The Holy Spirit, in love, unites the believer to God and to one another. To be filled with the Spirit is to be filled with love. The Holy Spirit is the source of the Church's life, love, unity, joy, and worship. The life and gifting of the Holy Spirit must be understood and pursued from the perspective of the Trinitarian life of God (1 Cor. 13).

I. **THE REVELATION OF GOD AS TRINITY IN UNITY**
    (Deut. 6:4-5; Mark 12:29-30; Matt. 28:19; 2 Cor. 13:14; 1 Peter 1:2; Jude 20-21; John 17:21)

    A. There is an important distinction between God as spirit and God as Holy Spirit. God as spirit refers to the nature or essence of God (John 4:24), while God as Holy Spirit refers to the divine person of the Holy Spirit. The first was well understood in the Old Testament, but not the second. Israel's relationship to God centered in God's disclosure of His oneness or unity. In contrast to the *polytheism* of Israel's neighbors, the Hebrews recognized Jehovah as their sole creator, their only deliverer, and the only one worthy of their love and worship (*monotheism*). The *Shema* is the heart of Jewish belief and worship and expresses Israel's belief in the oneness of God: "Hear, O Israel: The Lord our God, the Lord is one. Love the Lord your God with all your heart and with all your soul and with all your strength" (Deut. 6:4-5; see also Mark 12: 29-30).

B. The full revelation of the Holy Spirit in the Godhead did not occur in the Old Testament. But the Trinity was suggested in a number of ways. Two names for God (*Elohim* and *Adonai*) were plural in form but always accompanied by singular verbs and adjectives to emphasize God's unity. Some passages in the Old Testament prepared for the fuller Trinitarian revelation of God in the New Testament (e.g., Gen. 1:26; 3:22; 11:7; Ps. 110:1).

C. The words *holy spirit* are found in only two contexts in the Old Testament. In Psalm 51, David's prayer of repentance, he prays that God's "holy spirit" not be taken from him (v. 11). In Isaiah 63:10-11, the prophet speaks of God's graciousness in delivering the Israelites out of Egypt and putting His "holy spirit" in the midst of them. Yet, Isaiah says the people rebelled against God and grieved His "holy spirit" (v. 10). These texts were not referring to the Holy Spirit as divine person, but the spirit of God the Israelites knew to be holy in character. In the Old Testament, the Holy Spirit is generally referred to as "My Spirit" (Gen. 6:3), "the Spirit of God" (2 Chron. 15:1), "the Spirit of the Lord" (Isa. 11:2), and "the Spirit of the Sovereign God" (61:1).

D. The point is not that the Holy Spirit did not exist or was not active in the Old Testament. Rather, the divine person of the Holy Spirit was not fully known, though intimated in many ways. The full revelation of God as Trinity in Unity had to await the completion of God's self-disclosure in the New Testament. The climactic event was the resurrection of Jesus from the dead. This unique event authenticated that He was more than a prophet or a good man. He was indeed the Son of God. The Holy Spirit too was soon recognized as divine person. It became clear that what belongs to the Son belongs to the Spirit, and what belongs to the Spirit belongs to the Son (John 16:13-14). The divine persons were distinguished by speaking of the Father as the *unbegotten*, the Son as the *begotten*, and the Holy Spirit as *proceeding* (15:26). *To beget* is not to become a father in the sense of making something different, but in the sense of begetting something of the same kind as oneself. A human begets humans; animals beget animals; God begets God. Before anything was made, Christ was eternally begotten of the Father.

E. The triunity of God, clearly stated in the baptismal formula (Matt. 28:19) and the church's benediction (2 Cor. 13:14), together with associations of the Holy Spirit with the other persons of the Trinity (e.g., Luke 3:21-22; 1 Peter 1:1-2; Jude 20-21) eventually found its way into the ecumenical creeds of the church. At the *Council of Constantinople* in AD 381, the church confessed the Holy Spirit to be "the Lord and life-giver, proceeding from the Father, object of the same worship and the same glory with the Father and the Son." The Western churches later added the so-called *filioque* clause, adding that the Spirit proceeds "from the Son" as well as the Father.

F. There were major distortions and heresies regarding the Trinity in the early church. Virtually all these distortions still exist in various forms today. One, found in the writings of the so-called Cappadocian fathers, viewed the Trinity as three equal, independent, and autonomous beings. This view is known as *Tritheism* because in reality it recognizes three separate deities. When the church spoke of three divine *persons*, they did not mean there were three deities. They simply meant that Father, Son, and Holy Spirit exist in a reciprocal relationship that is personal in nature. Memory, understanding, and will, for example, are distinct aspects of our selfhood, but they are not separate and independent entities (Augustine).

The other extreme, associated with Sabellius and his followers, held that Father, Son, and Holy Spirit were merely different manifestations or names of God. This view is known as *Sabellianism*. At times God appears as Father, at times as Son, other times as Holy Spirit. But they are the same. This view protected the unity of God but denied a true Trinity. It was sometimes known as *modalism* and is today associated with "Jesus only" proponents.

Another view, *Arianism*, was associated with a churchman named Arius, who viewed the Son and Holy Spirit as lesser, subordinate beings the Father willed into existence for His purposes. In reality, the

Son and Holy Spirit were viewed as lesser forms of deity. This view still persists among Unitarians, Jehovah's Witnesses, and Mormons who hold the Son and Holy Spirit below the deity of the Father.

What the church was really intent on preserving was the view that in the oneness or unity of God there is a Trinitarian distinction of persons known as Father, Son, and Holy Spirit. They are not three individuals but three conscious distinctions within the one divine essence. The Father, as the fount of deity, is said to originate. The Son, eternally begotten of the Father, reveals. The Holy Spirit, eternally proceeding from the Father and the Son, executes the will of God. All that God wills to do, He does through the agency of the Holy Spirit.

The Triunity of God

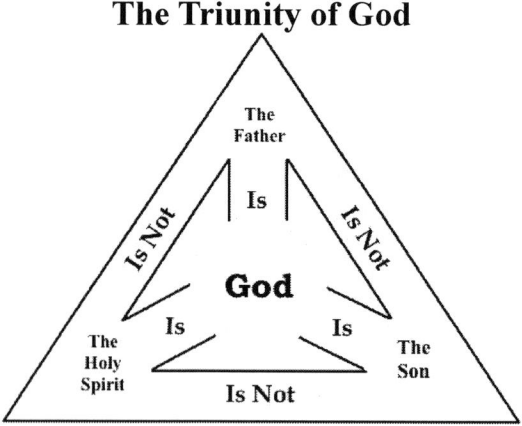

Eternal Relationship Between Father, Son, and Spirit

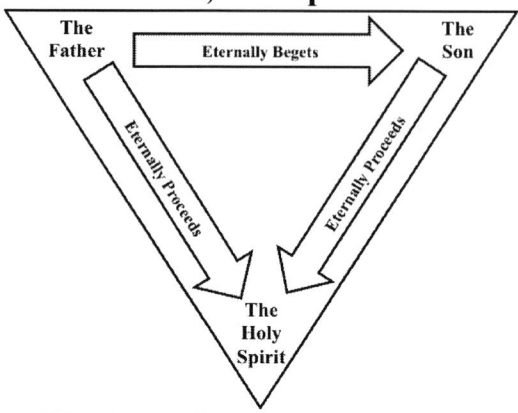

The Holy Spirit is the bond of love in the Trinity.

II. THE TRINITARIAN LIFE OF GOD
(1 John 4:8-9, 11-12; John 17; Rom. 5:5)

A. *God is love* (1 John 4:8). Father, Son, and Holy Spirit exist in an eternal relationship of shared love. Love originates in God and authenticates that we know God (vv. 11-12). What God is in Himself overflows in His going outside Himself for the world and for others. In this self-giving love that is of the very character of God, He creates the world and in love sends the Son as the atonement for our sins (1 John 4:9; John 3:16).

B. *Augustine* (AD 354-430), the great church father, taught in his work *On the Trinity* that the Holy Spirit is what is common to Father and Son. He is their shared love and holiness. The Father is only the Father of the Son. The Son is only the Son of the Father. The Spirit is what is common to Father and Son. He is the bond of love in the Trinity, the self-giving *agape* love that is shared with us through the Holy Spirit. Paul says, "God has poured out his love into our hearts by the Holy Spirit, whom he has given to us" (Rom. 5:5). It is common for Christians to think of the Holy Spirit as a mighty rushing wind, as purging fire, power, unction, as the One who reproves and convicts, while minimizing the great truth that the very essence of the Holy Spirit is love. To be filled with the Holy Spirit is to be filled with holy love. William Seymour, father of the modern Pentecostal Movement, rightly believed that the strongest evidence one is filled with the Holy Spirit is a life of love.

III. THE LIFE AND MINISTRY OF THE CHURCH
(John 17)

A. There is an important practical truth that all Christians should know regarding the relation of the Trinity to God's ongoing work in the Church and the world. God's purpose and work in the world and the Church flow out of the inner life of the Trinity. What we know about God and His triune nature informs our understanding of what kind of people He wills for His church, for we have been, above all else, called to godliness.

B. Tradition teaches that Catholicism has been primarily concerned with the church's structure and Protestantism with its message. What has been too often lacking in both is the life of the Church made possible through the Holy Spirit. Worship, inspired by the Holy Spirit, is the life of the Church. Through its worship, the Church witnesses to the resurrected Lord who lives in His church through the Holy Spirit. Jesus told the woman at the well in Samaria that true worshipers must worship God in spirit and in truth (John 4:24).

C. Just as the Holy Spirit is the bond of love and unity in the Godhead, He is the basis of love and unity in the Church. In the communion of the body of Christ, the Spirit brings believers together into participation with the life and love of the Godhead. This is the *koinonia* of the body participating together in the life of Christ through the Spirit.

D. From the relational essence of God, we know God has created us as social beings and intends our loving interaction with Him and with others. This is not only the basis of our joy and prayer life but our service as well. The gifting of the Holy Spirit, and the purpose of the gifts, which is to edify others, is to be understood from the interrelationship that exists in the Trinity where all glorify one another. Whatever gifts or ministry one may have, that which is necessary to the building up of the body of Christ is a willingness to serve others. Love manifests itself in service to others, the only office in the Church to which all Christians are called. The marks of greatness in God's kingdom are humility and service. Jesus is the model for the Church: "Who, though he was in the form of God [preexistent and divine], did not count equality with God a thing to be grasped, but emptied himself, taking the form of a servant, being born in the likeness of men" (Phil. 2:5-7 RSV).

LIFE APPLICATION

H. Wheeler Robinson, a leader and scholar among Evangelicals, tells how during a serious illness he was brought to ask himself why the truths of evangelical Christianity that he had preached to others now failed to bring him personal strength. "They seemed true," he said, "but they lacked vitality. The image that presented itself to me was that of a great balloon, with ample lifting power if only one had the strength to grasp the rope that railed down from it." The result of this experience, Robinson says, was that it led him to seek for what was missing in his conception of evangelical truth. "I found it," he confessed, "in my neglect of the Holy Spirit in which the New Testament is so rich."

As Robinson discovered, it is not enough for the church to have the truth on ice. The truth of the gospel needs always to be set aflame by the presence and power of the Holy Spirit. A doctrine of the Holy Spirit alone is not enough. We continually need the Holy Spirit to fill our lives with the same life, love, and joy that exist in the interior life of the Trinity. Only then will our evangelical doctrines have conviction and power.

What about you? Are you allowing the Holy Spirit to give life and vitality to you and the things you believe? If not, ask Him to give you the life and strength you need. The Holy Spirit can bring your Christian experience alive and give you a renewed love and joy in Jesus Christ.

DISCUSSION

The Revelation of God as Trinity in Unity
1. Do you agree that the Trinity is clearly suggested in the Old Testament but not fully revealed? Explain.
2. What language did the church find in the Scriptures that allowed them to make a distinction between Father, Son, and Holy Spirit? Can you explain what this language means?
3. Explain the fundamental errors in Tritheism, Sabellianism, and Arianism. What is necessary to be said in order to preserve an orthodox view of the Trinity?

The Trinitarian Life of God
1. What does it mean to you to say that the Holy Spirit is the bond of love in the Trinity?
2. What is meant by referring to Father, Son, and Holy Spirit as "persons"?
3. Talk about the overflowing of God's love into creation and redemption.

The Life and Ministry of the Church
1. How does the work of the Holy Spirit in the Trinity manifest itself in the life and ministry of the Church? Be specific.
2. Why is truth alone not enough in the Church?
3. Explain why the gifts of the Spirit need to be understood and pursued from the perspective of the Trinitarian life of God.

GLOSSARY OF TERMS/CONCEPTS

Arius/Arianism: A fourth-century churchman who taught that because God is one, neither Jesus nor the Holy Spirit could have been fully divine. Arius and his followers (Arians) regarded the Son as the highest created being of God, thus a lesser deity. This teaching was condemned at the Council of Nicea in AD 325.

Augustine/On the Trinity: One of the great theologians among the church fathers. In his treatise *On the Trinity*, Augustine expounded the view that the Spirit is the bond of love and unity between Father and Son. The Holy Spirit likewise bonds believers to God and to other believers in the body of Christ.

Council of Constantinople (AD 381): The council that refuted the Arian heresy and formulated the orthodox doctrine of the Trinity.

Filioque: A Latin term that means "and the Son." The phrase was added to the Constantinopolitan Creed (AD 381) by the Western churches in the sixth century. In essence, the phrase acknowledges that the Holy Spirit proceeds from the Son as well as the Father. Because it did not have the consensus of the Eastern churches, it ignited a controversy that eventually contributed to the split between the Roman Catholic and Greek Orthodox churches in AD 1054.

Persons: The reference to Father, Son, and Holy Spirit as divine persons does not mean they are three individual beings. Rather, the Father, Son, and Holy Spirit are personable and relational in their essence.

Polytheism/Monotheism: *Polytheism* is belief in or worship of more than one God; *Monotheism* is the belief that there is only one God.

Sabellianism: The view of Sabellius, an early third-century figure who taught that God is revealed successively in salvation history as Father (Creator and Lawgiver), as Son (Redeemer), and finally as Holy Spirit (Sustainer and Giver of Grace). The error in this view was its denial of a true distinction of persons. Hence, no true Trinity. The view holds to a trinity of revelation but not three real distinctions. This view is often referred to as *modalism*.

Shema: From the Hebrew word for "hear," "Hear O Israel: The Lord our God, the Lord is one" (Deut. 6:4).

Tritheism: The erroneous view that the Trinity consists of three equal, independent, and autonomous beings, each of whom is divine. This view can be found in subtle form in the writings of the Cappadocian fathers of the fourth century.

Unbegotten/begotten/proceeds: The Father is the fount of deity, the unbegotten; the Son is begotten of the Father. This does not mean "made" or "created," but begetting something of the same kind. Humans beget humans; animals beget animals; deity begets deity. The Son is eternally begotten of the Father. The Holy Spirit eternally proceeds (is generated) from the Father and Son.

RESOURCES FOR ADDITIONAL STUDY

Arrington, French L. *Christian Doctrine: A Pentecostal Perspective.* Vol. 1. Cleveland, Tenn.: Pathway, 1992.

Brumback, Carl. *God in Three Persons.* Cleveland, Tenn.: Pathway, 1959.

Finlayson, R. A. "Trinity," in *New Bible Dictionary.* Grand Rapids: Eerdmans, 1962.

Horton, Stanley. *What the Bible Says About the Holy Spirit.* Springfield, Mo.: Gospel Publishing, 1976.

Little, Paul E. "Our Triune God," in *Know What You Believe.* Wheaton, Ill.: Victor, 1989.

McGrath, Alister. *Christian Theology.* Oxford: Blackburn, 1994.

Pinnock, Charles H. *Flame of Love: A Theology of the Holy Spirit.* Downers Grove, Ill.: InterVarsity, 1996.

Lesson 3

The Holy Spirit in the Old Testament

As noted in lesson 2, Christian reflection on the Trinity grows out of the New Testament witness to the presence and activity of God in Christ through the Holy Spirit. The whole process of salvation bears witness to the activity of Father, Son, and Holy Spirit. In the economy of salvation we see the distinct yet related roles of the divine persons in the Trinity.

In this lesson we turn our attention to the manner in which the Holy Spirit is made known in the historical process, particularly in the Old Testament, where we can discern four major emphases: (l) the work of the Spirit in Creation; (2) the Spirit as God's power to save and deliver, to gift and equip for divine service, and for judgment; (3) the Spirit as the giver of prophetic speech; and (4) the foretelling by the prophets of the coming of the Messiah (Isaiah), a new covenant (Ezekiel), and the coming of the Spirit in prophetic and charismatic power (Joel). Each of these promises involves a special work of the Holy Spirit, which we will discuss in a later lesson.

I. THE SPIRIT AS CREATOR AND LIFE GIVER
(Gen. 1:2; 2:7; Ps. 33:6; Job 33:4; 34:14-15; Ezek. 37:5; Rom. 8:11; John 6:63)

A. The Hebrew word for *Spirit* is *ruach*. It is a word with many shades of meaning, but is most often translated as "breath" and "wind." Both terms help us understand the work and ministry of the Holy Spirit in the Old Testament.

B. *Ruach* means "breath," and refers to the breath of God that brings forth life, creates, sustains, and renews. Like an artist who desires to create out of a creative impulse, God is disposed to create out of the overflowing love that exists in the Godhead. In the Trinitarian life of God there is an eternal giving and sharing of life. The Spirit opens up this inter-Trinitarian relationship to the world, creating through the power of the Word.

The Spirit of God moved upon the waters, bringing forth an ordered cosmos out of chaos, light out of darkness, habitation out of desolation, human life in the image of God (Gen. 1:2; 2:7). The psalmist said, "By the word of the Lord were the heavens made, their starry host by the breath [*ruach*] of his mouth" (33:6). Job likewise acknowledged, "The Spirit of God has made me; the breath [*ruach*] of the Almighty gives me life" (Job 33:4). The Spirit that creates, Job notes, is the Spirit that preserves our lives: "If it were his intention and he withdrew his spirit and breath [*ruach*], all humanity would perish together and man would return to the dust" (34:14-15).

The Spirit that creates and preserves life also restores life to the lifeless. Ezekiel's vision of dry bones is a graphic picture of God's power to bring life out of death when breathed upon by God's Spirit (Ezek. 37:5). What happened to a lifeless and hopeless nation exiled in Babylon, also happens to those who are dead in trespasses and sin, when breathed upon by he Spirit of God. And, the resurrection of Jesus Christ from the dead also assures us that the Spirit will give resurrection life to all who are indwelt by the Spirit when Christ appears (Rom. 8:11). Jesus said: "The Spirit gives life" (John 6:63).

II. THE SPIRIT AS GOD'S POWER TO SAVE, EQUIP FOR SERVICE, AND JUDGE
(Judg. 6:34; 11:29; 13:25; 14:6, 19; 1 Sam. 10:6, 10; 11:6; Zech. 4:6; Acts 2:2)

A. In the Old Testament, the Spirit of God [*ruach*] is also likened to "wind," a metaphor for divine power and energy. Like the powerful desert winds in the Middle East, the power of God's Spirit moves to save, equip for God's service, and judge those who oppose God and His purpose.

B. It was the power of the wind that saved the fleeing Hebrews from the Egyptians at the Red Sea. The wind of deliverance that saved the Hebrews brought judgment on the pursuing Egyptians who were drowned in the sea. During the time of the judges, the Spirit of God came mightily upon Israel's leaders to save God's people from their enemies. We read that the Spirit of God "took possession" of Gideon to rally the Israelites against the Amalekites (Judg. 6:34 NLT). Through the power of the Spirit, Jephthah was given a great victory over the Ammonites (11:29). Young Samson was "stirred up" and given supernatural strength (13:25; 14:6, 19).

King Saul was "changed into a different person" and prophesied through the power of the Spirit (1 Sam. 10:6, 10). When the Spirit came upon Saul, his anger was kindled against the enemies of Israel and the people were gathered for battle (11:6). When God chose to save and deliver His people, His mighty power (wind) blew against the enemies of God.

C. The prophet Zechariah reminded Zerubbabel that the work of God could not be accomplished through human strategy or might. It could only be done in the power of the Spirit: "This is the word of the Lord to Zerubbabel: 'Not by might nor by power, but by my Spirit.' says the Lord Almighty" (Zech. 4:6). We will see this same emphasis in the New Testament. Jesus accomplished what the Father had sent Him to do in the power of the Holy Spirit (Luke 4:14). And it was through the power of the Spirit (symbolized by the "rushing mighty wind" of Pentecost, KJV) that the early church carried out the Great Commission (Acts 2:2). The Church needs always to be reminded that God is offended at our attempts to achieve through human might and strategy what can only be accomplished in the power of the Holy Spirit.

D. The arm of flesh was not Israel's hope, nor is it ours. When God chooses and calls us, He also equips us for His service. Our natural abilities and skills are never enough; God's work must be done in the power of His Spirit. He never leaves the accomplishment of His will to the level of our abilities. This great truth was amplified over and over as God raised up leaders in Israel through whom the Spirit of the Lord could work: patriarchs, judges, prophets, craftsmen, priests, and kings who were anointed by the Spirit for divine service.

III. GIFTS AND MINISTRIES OF THE SPIRIT
(Gen. 41:38; Num. 11:10-30; Deut. 34:9; Ex. 31:1-11; 2 Tim. 3:16; Zech. 7:12; 1 Sam. 16:13-14; Ps. 51:11)

A. The patriarchs were gifted and moved upon by the Spirit of God. Even the pharaoh recognized that Joseph was a man in whom the Spirit dwelled (Gen. 41:38). In Joseph's case, the working of the Spirit was noted with regard to his ability to interpret dreams.

The Spirit was upon Moses, equipping him with a special ability to deliver and lead Israel during their wilderness wanderings. It was a challenging responsibility, and Moses learned that leadership is a difficult task, especially when the people are rebellious and do not want to be led. When the burden of leadership became too great, God placed the Spirit that had rested on Moses upon seventy elders who assisted Moses in leading the people and handling their problems (Num. 11:10-30). The primary authority still rested with Moses, but the task of leadership did not rest upon a single individual. The Spirit taught Moses a two-pronged lesson that all spiritual leaders should know: Leadership in the body of Christ is a shared responsibility, and all who lead need the anointing and gifting of the Spirit.

After the death of Moses, leadership fell to Joshua, who is described as a man "filled with the spirit of wisdom" (Deut. 34:9). Even the craftsmen Bezalel and Oholiab, who were charged with the responsibility for building the Tabernacle and making the garments for the high priest of Israel, were equipped for their task by the Spirit of God, who gave them special knowledge, intelligence, and ability (Ex. 31:1-11).

B. In 1 Samuel, attention is given to the anointing of kings. Anointing oil was a symbol of the Spirit. When Samuel anointed David, the Spirit of the Lord came upon David, while the Spirit departed from Saul (16:13-14). We are told that when the Spirit of the Lord departed from Saul, an "evil spirit from the Lord tormented him." This has been a difficult scripture to understand for many, because we know that God is not the source of evil. However, because Saul had rebelled against God, he was given over to demonic influence. Just as Samson's strength was withdrawn because of his disobedience, the Spirit of God was withdrawn from Saul when he chose to disobey the Lord. The same Spirit that empowers and blesses can be withdrawn and experienced as a form of judgment and wrath. What David feared most after his sins of adultery and murder was that God would withdraw His Spirit from him (Ps. 51:11). What happens to individuals can also happen to churches and institutions when God's Spirit has been withdrawn.

C. The Spirit of God was especially linked to the gift of *prophecy*. The word *prophet* (*nali*) means one who speaks for another, specifically one who communicates the divine will. Prophets were God's messengers, anointed by the Spirit of the Lord to deliver "inspired speech" to the people. The apostle Paul wrote to Timothy that the Old Testament Scriptures were trustworthy and profitable because they were inspired by the Holy Spirit (2 Tim. 3:16). From the time of the first great prophet Moses, until the last great prophets Haggai, Zechariah, and Malachi, the Lord raised up prophets in Israel. He put His words in their mouth and fulfilled His word through the power of His Spirit (Zech. 7:12). Everything inspired by the Spirit is not contained in the canon of Scripture, but everything contained in Scripture was inspired by the Spirit of God. In fact, the Spirit of God and the prophetic word were so closely united, that when the last prophets were gone, it was generally assumed that the Spirit of God had departed and would not return until the coming of the Messiah.

Prophets were not called to deliver their own message or speak on their own authority, but to speak the word of the Lord. Statements like "Thus says the Lord" or "The word of the Lord came to me, saying" usually prefaced their message. Sometimes the word from God was a word regarding future events, but more often it was a word for a present situation. Prophets received their message in different ways (dreams, visions, ecstasies, miracles, etc.), and they sometimes communicated the message of God through unusual events, like a locust invasion, a drought, a burning bush, or the work of a potter. Some of Israel's hymns were prophetic, given to the accompaniment of music. Elijah and Elisha were leaders of a band of prophets known as "the school of the prophets" at Bethel, Jericho, and Gilgal. Whatever the form of the message or the demeanor of the prophet, the distinguishing mark of the true prophet of God was the anointing and inspiration of the Spirit of God. This was the source of their message and the sign of their authenticity.

It is important to note that while prophesying was a sign of the presence of the Spirit, it was not necessarily an endorsement of the prophet's character. God used Balaam to deliver His message despite his flawed character. The Spirit continued to work through King Saul even after his actions were clearly displeasing to God (1 Sam. 19:24). This is another important lesson to be learned. The fact that one prophesies or even does mighty works does not necessarily mean that person is pleasing to God or living in right relationship with Him. Godly character is determined by what the Word of God teaches, not by charismatic activity or mighty works. God is sovereign. He can use whoever and whatever He wills for

His purpose (including the devil), but this does not mean that person's character is right with God. Jesus said, "Many will say to me on that day, 'Lord, Lord, did we not prophesy in your name, and in your name drive out demons and perform many miracles?' Then I will tell them plainly, 'I never knew you. Away from me, you evildoers!'" (Matt. 7:22-23).

IV. THE HOLY SPIRIT IN ISRAEL'S FUTURE
(Ps. 137:1-6; Ezek. 37:1-14; Isa. 7:14; 9:6-7; 11:2; 42:1; 61:1-2; Luke 4:16-20; Lev. 25:10-13; Ezek. 36:25-27; John 3:5; Titus 3:5; Joel 2:28-29)

A. During their Babylonian exile, the nation of Israel was at its lowest point. Jerusalem had fallen. The Temple had been destroyed. Only a small remnant remained in the land. There was no song in the hearts of the people. "By the rivers of Babylon," the psalmist recorded, "we sat and wept when we remembered Zion" (137:1). It was during the time of their deepest despair that God gave the prophets a word of hope for the nation's future. There was an inspired awareness that God had a plan and purpose for His people. Jeremiah assured the people that God had a dream, a vision, and a purpose for His people; He would not forsake them (Jer. 29:10-14). Ezekiel prophesied a future when the Spirit of God would give renewed life to the nation and redirect the hearts of the people to God (Ezek. 37:1-14). The hope of Israel rested upon three specific promises given by Isaiah, Ezekiel, and Joel, each of which involved a special work of the Holy Spirit.

B. The promise given to Isaiah centered in the coming of the *Messiah*. The expectation that grew up concerning a messiah did not center on a divine figure but a human deliverer, someone like King David, upon whom the Spirit of God would rest. God would especially favor the Messiah, or "Anointed One."

Isaiah 7:14 is quite specific about the Messiah. He would be a sign to those who put their trust in the Lord, a virgin-born Son whose name would be *Immanuel*, meaning "God with us" (Matt. 1:23). The government would be on His shoulders. He would establish the throne of David forever. He would be called "Wonderful Counselor, Mighty God, Everlasting Father, Prince of Peace" (Isa. 9:6-7). He would manifest the gifts of an ideal king: "the Spirit of wisdom and of understanding, the Spirit of counsel and of power, the Spirit of knowledge and of the fear of the Lord" (11:2). The distinguishing mark of the Messiah would be the permanent resting of the Spirit of God upon Him. The Messiah would inaugurate the long-awaited kingdom of God on earth. It would be a time when God's Anointed Servant would bring forth a perfect understanding of God's law and restore justice to the nations (42:1).

The coming of the Anointed Servant would be a new beginning for Israel, a time of blessing and favor for all. It would be a time of even greater joy and hope than the *Year of Jubilee*, when God's ownership and lordship of all things were celebrated (Lev. 25:10-13). The liberation inaugurated by the Messiah would bring freedom from injustice and oppression. It would release the blessings and favor God desired for His people. Isaiah described what would happen through the Spirit-anointed Messiah: "The Spirit of the Sovereign Lord is on me, because the Lord has anointed me to preach good news to the poor. He has sent me to bind up the brokenhearted, to proclaim freedom for the captives and release from darkness for the prisoners, to proclaim the year of the Lord's favor and the day of vengeance of our God, to comfort all who mourn" (61:1-2; cf. Luke 4:16-19).

C. The prophecy of Ezekiel centered in a *new covenant*, a covenant God would establish in the hearts of the people, not on tables of stone. He spoke of a time when the people of God would have a new sensitivity to God, when they would be obedient to God and His statutes because He had put His Spirit in them. It would be a day when the Spirit would indwell the people, when they would be changed from the inside out: "I will give you a new heart and put a new spirit in you; I will remove from you your heart of stone and give you a heart of flesh. And I will put my Spirit in you and move you to follow my decrees, and be careful to keep my laws" (Ezek. 36:26-27).

Ezekiel's promise was what we know in the New Testament as *regeneration*, or the *new birth* that Jesus taught Nicodemus (John 3:5). The apostle Paul referred to this experience as our being saved "by the washing of regeneration and renewing by the Holy Spirit" (Titus 3:5 NASB). Ezekiel was foretelling God's desire to cleanse our temple for the indwelling presence of the Holy Spirit. Just as God dwelt in

His holy Temple in the Old Testament, there was a time coming when He would indwell a holy people.

D. Joel's prophecy represented something different but complementary. Moses, the first great prophet, longed for a time when the Spirit of God would turn all of God's people into prophets (Num. 11:29). The work of the Spirit in the Old Testament, for the most part, was limited to Israel's spiritual leaders and their tasks. Joel, the prophet of Pentecost, prophesied that a day was coming when that would change. The Spirit of God would be poured out in prophetic power on all flesh: "I will pour out my Spirit on all people. Your sons and daughters will prophesy, your old men will dream dreams, your young men will see visions. Even on my servants, both men and women, I will pour out my Spirit in those days" (Joel 2:28-29). Moses' desire that God's people would be an empowered prophetic community finally would come to pass.

Unlike Ezekiel, who foresaw the work of the Spirit in relation to conversion and a new covenant (a Pauline emphasis), Joel prophesied that the Spirit would manifest His prophetic ministry in extraordinary power and charismatic activity (a Lukan emphasis). The coming of the Spirit would turn God's covenant people into a prophetic community bearing witness to Jesus Christ. They would do so without regard to social status (servants and handmaidens), gender (sons and daughters), or age (young and old). The prophecies of Ezekiel and Joel were about different, but complementary, and vital ministries of the Holy Spirit. In future lessons we will consider both of these emphases.

LIFE APPLICATION

Several years ago when my wife and I were serving a Bible school in Europe, we made frequent trips to and from Germany. I noticed that the flight from Germany to Atlanta took about two hours longer than the flight from Atlanta to Stuttgart. When I inquired as to why one trip took considerably more time than the other, though they were the same distance, I was informed that it was because of the wind. Flying east across the Atlantic, we enjoyed a tailwind; returning, we had to fly into a headwind. It was the same wind, but one that was experienced differently depending on whether it was at our back or in our face.

This taught me an important spiritual lesson. When our lives are going in the direction in which the wind of God's Spirit is blowing, we are blessed and favored. But when our lives are turned into the force of the wind, we experience it as opposition and struggle. Water and wind in the Old Testament were symbols of the Holy Spirit. The power of the wind and rain that blew into Israel from the Mediterranean Sea brought cool breezes and much-needed rain. The wind blowing in from the desert to the east, on the other hand, frequently brought sandstorms and oppressive heat.

The prophets Hosea, Joel, and Zechariah spoke of the rain, brought by the western winds, that refreshed the land and brought a harvest of life and blessing (Hos. 6:3; Joel 2:23-32; Zech. 10:1). They spoke of the "former rain" (Joel 2:23 KJV), or autumn rain, that came at the time of plowing and planting. These rains prepared the ground for the seed, much like the rain and wind of Pentecost prepared the church for sowing the gospel seed (Acts 2:14-21; Joel 2:28-32). The "latter rain," or spring rain, came when the fields were ready for harvest, preparing the grain for the reapers, much like the wind and rain of the Spirit that has been poured out in these last days.

To live in accordance with the will and purpose of God is to enjoy His blessings and favor, but to oppose what God is doing through His Spirit is to invite death and destruction. Fierce sandstorms created by hot desert winds could destroy and reshape everything in their path. Mighty Babylon, Isaiah said, was like withered grass and flowers before the breath of the Lord (40:7-8). In the New Testament we read about Ananias and his wife, Sapphira, who encountered God's judgment when they turned their deceitful intentions into the face of the wind that was blowing in the early church (Acts 5:1-11). To move in the direction of the wind of the Spirit is to enjoy God's favor, but to oppose the work of the Spirit of God is to invite spiritual death and destruction.

DISCUSSION
The Spirit as Creator and Life-Giver
1. How does the Hebrew word for *Spirit* (*ruach*) help us understand the work of the Spirit in the Old Testament?
2. Discuss this statement: "God is eternally disposed to create, to share His overflowing love with the world."

The Spirit as God's Power to Save, Equip for Service, and Judge
1. Discuss the statement: "God never leaves the accomplishment of His will to the level of our abilities."
2. Also, discuss: "With the calling of God for a task comes an anointing and gifting to do that for which we have been called."

God With *Us and* In *Us*

Gifts and Ministries of the Spirit
1. What did Moses learn about leadership that we should know and practice today?
2. Describe what it meant to be a prophet of God in the Old Testament.

The Holy Spirit in Israel's Future
1. Explain what Isaiah prophesied concerning the coming Messiah and the Spirit of God.
2. What was Ezekiel's message concerning Israel's future?
3. How does Joel's prophecy relate to what happened on the Day of Pentecost?

GLOSSARY OF TERMS/CONCEPTS

Economic Trinity: Refers to the Trinity in relationship to the world, particularly with regard to the outworking of God's plan (economy) of salvation.

Messiah: A Hebrew term meaning "Anointed One." The Israelites came to anticipate a person anointed by the Spirit who would function as king and priest over Israel.

New Covenant: God's covenant with believers through Jesus Christ. The New Testament, or new covenant, is all about those who place their trust in Jesus Christ and come under the benefits of the covenant of grace.

Prophet: One who announces or pours forth the declaration of God. It was through the Spirit of God the prophets received the divine communication.

Ruach: The Hebrew word for *Spirit*. It has many shades of meaning but is most generally translated as "breath" (i.e., life) and "wind" (i.e., power).

Year of Jubilee: The Year of Jubilee was celebrated in Israel every fifty years. God's purpose in instituting this special year was to guarantee justice and to keep the rich from accumulating wealth and land at the expense of the disadvantaged.

RESOURCES FOR ADDITIONAL STUDY

Horton, Stanley. *What the Bible Says About the Holy Spirit*. Springfield, Mo.: Gospel Publishing, 1976.

McGrath, Alister. *Christian Theology*. Oxford: Blackburn, 1994.

Moltmann, Jurgen. *The Spirit of Life: A Universal Affirmation*. Minneapolis: Fortress, 1992.

Sims, John. *Power With Purpose*. Cleveland, Tenn.: Pathway, 1984.

Lesson 4

The Holy Spirit in the Life and Ministry of Jesus

The story of Jesus in the New Testament has two foci regarding His person. The first focus is on Jesus as Son of God: "In the beginning was the Word, and the Word was with God, and the Word was God. . . . The Word became flesh and made his dwelling among us" (John 1:1, 14). The second focus is on the humanity of Jesus and His work in the power of the Holy Spirit. Peter describes Jesus as "Jesus of Nazareth . . . a man accredited by God to you by miracles, wonders and signs, which God did among you through him" (Acts 2:22). He likewise describes Jesus as a man "anointed [by God] . . . with the Holy Spirit and power, [who] went around doing good and healing all who were under the power of the devil, because God was with him" (10:38).

These are not antithetical but complementary emphases, even though one focuses on the divine person of Jesus while the other emphasizes His Spirit-anointed life and ministry as the Christ of God. Throughout the Gospel narratives, the Spirit is actively working in every aspect of Jesus' life and ministry. Irenaeus (AD 130-200), an early church father, emphasized the role of both the Son and the Spirit in the redemptive plan by referring to them as the "two hands of God." Both were sent by God to complete the work of redemption. As we focus on their symbiotic relationship in this lesson, two major emphases will be highlighted: (1) the Holy Spirit in the mission and ministry of Jesus; and (2) the Holy Spirit in the message of Jesus.

I. THE SPIRIT AND JESUS
(Luke 1:35; Gen. 1:2; Luke 2:27; Matt. 3:16; Luke 4:1, 14, 18-19; Heb. 9:14; Rom. 1:3-4; 8:11; 1 Cor. 15:45; 1 Peter 3:18; 2 Peter 1:4)

A. The roots of the idea that the Spirit would rest upon Jesus and that He would be the bearer of the Holy Spirit are in the Old Testament. As noted in the previous lesson, Isaiah prophesied that the Messiah would be "anointed" by the Spirit of God. Joel prophesied that in the last days, the age of the Messiah, there would be a special outpouring of the Spirit on all flesh. As foretold by the prophets, every aspect of the life and ministry of Jesus was Spirit-anointed. The Spirit of the Lord, working through Jesus the Christ (i.e., the Anointed One), opened up to the human race a redemptive relationship with God. Through the redemptive work of the Son, empowered by the Spirit, provision was made for all to be restored that had been lost through Adam.

B. The story of Jesus is everywhere filled with the joint ministry of the Son and the Spirit. Jesus' miraculous conception was by the Holy Spirit (Matt. 1:18-20). The angel told Mary that the Holy Spirit would come upon her, and that the power of the Most High would overshadow her (Luke 1:35). The language used is reminiscent of Genesis 1:2, where it is said the Spirit hovered over the waters at creation. Luke is, in actuality, telling us that God is at work bringing about a new creation through Jesus.

In the Temple a devout man named Simeon, who was waiting for the deliverer of Israel, was moved upon by the Spirit to recognize and bless the baby Jesus (Luke 2:27). When John baptized Jesus in the Jordan River, the Holy Spirit descended upon Jesus in bodily form like a dove, symbolic of the messianic age and the renewal of creation that Jesus would bring through the life and power of the Spirit (Matt. 3:16). One will recall that it was the dove that brought Noah and his family hope for a renewed creation. What God was doing through Jesus of Nazareth, in the power of the life-giving Spirit, would restore God's image in His people and, in due time, bring about a new created order.

"Full of the Holy Spirit," Jesus was led (literally "driven") by the Spirit into the wilderness, where He was tempted by the devil for forty days and nights (Luke 4:1). The Spirit does not always save us from temptation and opposition from the Enemy, but uses it to prepare us for the purpose God has for us. During the time of His preparation for ministry in the wilderness, Jesus depended on the Spirit, as we must, to help Him deal with the temptations of Satan. Following this time in the wilderness, Jesus returned to Galilee "in the power of the Spirit" (v. 14), where His ministry began in earnest. In the synagogue at Nazareth, Jesus took the scroll containing the writing of Isaiah and read concerning Himself: "The Spirit of the Lord is on me, because he has anointed me to preach good news to the poor. He has sent me to proclaim freedom for the prisoners and recovery of sight for the blind, to release the oppressed, to proclaim the year of the Lord's favor" (Luke 4:18-19; cf. Isa. 61:1-2). The "year of the Lord's favor" was language associated with the Old Testament Year of Jubilee (Lev. 25). The passage Jesus read referred to God's promised end-time salvation, the establishing of the kingdom of God. "Today," Jesus said, "this scripture is fulfilled in your hearing" (Luke 4:21), indicating that God's rule and reign had truly come in Jesus, who was the Christ. Throughout His earthly ministry, the anointing and power of the Spirit was upon Jesus without measure as He preached and taught the good news of the Kingdom. In the power of the Spirit, Jesus performed signs and wonders that authenticated the presence of the Kingdom—healing the sick, raising the dead, and casting out unclean spirits.

When the time had come, Jesus traveled to Jerusalem where He would be rejected, suffer, and be crucified for the sins of the world in accordance with what Isaiah had prophesied (Isa. 53). The divine purpose that had been at work throughout His life would come to completion through His death and resurrection. As the apostle Paul described it, Jesus "was delivered over to death for our sins and was raised to life for our justification" (Rom. 4:25). God, for our sakes, allowed the suffering of Jesus into the triune life so suffering would not be alien to the Godhead. The Spirit that empowered Jesus to submit to the total will of the Father in Gethsemane empowered Jesus as He "offered himself unblemished to God" (Heb. 9:14). One cannot speak meaningfully of Jesus' death on the cross apart from His resurrection from the dead. It is the heart and center of the gospel message. Jesus acted vicariously on our behalf, not only by dying but also in rising from the dead (Rom. 5:10; Col. 2:12; 2 Tim. 1:10). The resurrection of Jesus, through the power of the Holy Spirit, was God's declaration that Jesus Christ is the Son of God (Rom. 1:3-4). This event, above all others, validated the work and divine nature of Jesus.

The Resurrection put aside all thoughts that Jesus was merely a prophetic or charismatic figure "adopted" by God and endowed with the gift of the Spirit. The empty tomb does not allow the presence of the Spirit in Jesus to lapse into some form of *adoptionism*, as some have advocated. In his letter to the Romans, Paul explains that the Spirit that was in Jesus has significance for us: "If the

Spirit of him who raised Jesus from the dead is living in you, he who raised Christ from the dead will also give life to your mortal bodies through his Spirit, who lives in you" (8:11). Through His resurrection, Jesus was transformed to the life of the age to come by the power of the Holy Spirit and has become, Paul says, "a life-giving spirit" (1 Cor. 15:45).

The Holy Spirit appropriates the redemptive work of Christ to the believer and draws us into union with Him. Our salvation is more than a legal matter, a changing of our standing before God (i.e., justification). It is participation in the life and glory of God through the Spirit. As the apostle Peter says, the Spirit brings us into the life of God so we can participate in the divine nature (1 Peter 3:18; 2 Peter 1:4).

II. THE HOLY SPIRIT IN THE MESSAGE OF JESUS
(Luke 11:20; Rom. 14:17; Matt. 28:19; 12:28-32; Isa. 42:1-4; Matt. 12:18; John 16:8-15; 14:16; 20:21-22; Acts 1:8; Luke 24:46-49)

A. The central message of Jesus was the *kingdom of God*. Jesus acknowledged a future dimension of the Kingdom that He would bring to pass at His return, but it was clear that Jesus was inaugurating the Kingdom in the power of His words and deeds through the Spirit of God. In answer to those who doubted, Jesus said, "If I drive out demons by the finger of God, then the kingdom of God has come to you" (Luke 11:20). The Holy Spirit is the substance and power of the Kingdom. Paul wrote to the Romans: "For the kingdom of God is not a matter of eating and drinking, but of righteousness, peace and joy in the Holy Spirit" (14:17). The story of Jesus in the Gospels is everywhere filled with the joint ministry of the Son and the Spirit.

B. Jesus taught His disciples many things about the Holy Spirit. He instructed them to baptize believers in the name of the triune God: Father, Son, and Holy Spirit (Matt. 28:19). He taught them the Spirit must not be *blasphemed* (i.e., knowingly attributing the work of the Spirit to evil). He who refuses to be saved through the work of the Holy Spirit cannot be saved at all (12:28-32). Whoever rejects the forgiveness the Spirit offers can expect to encounter the judgment of God (cf. Isa. 42:1-4; Matt. 12:18).

In Jesus' *parting discourse*, He taught His disciples the work of the Spirit in relation to unbelievers, believers, and the world. The Spirit, Jesus said, will reprove (i.e., convict, expose, refute, convince) the world of sin, righteousness, and judgment (John 16:8-15). The Spirit exposes and reproves sin to awaken in us a consciousness of sin and the need for forgiveness. The Spirit reveals Jesus Christ as the righteous Son of God and the only standard of true righteousness. The judgment of God is certain for all who reject the love and grace offered in Christ. Those who deny these truths cannot be of the Holy Spirit.

With regard to believers, Jesus taught that the Spirit dwells in us, guides us into truth, shows us things to come, and glorifies Christ. The indwelling Spirit is our helper, comforter, and advocate (i.e., *paraclete*; 14:16). The term *paraclete*, often translated as "comforter," means one that "comes alongside" of another to help in time of need. Jesus assured His disciples that when He returned to the Father, they would not be left without a divine helper. Jesus had been their helper and counselor while He was with them; He would be with them through the Spirit until the end of the age. Like Jesus' disciples, we do not know all we will need for the future. We have not encountered all that is still before us. But we can rest in the peace and confidence that the Holy Spirit will be our sufficiency regardless of what the future holds.

C. Much of what Jesus said about the ministry of the Holy Spirit centered in the disciples' mission. Jesus promised that they would be filled with the power of the Spirit to be His (Jesus') witnesses. They were called and empowered by the Spirit for the primary purpose of bearing witness to Jesus Christ and His kingdom. It is instructive to note that the first act of the risen Lord was to breathe the Spirit on His disciples and send them forth (John 20:21-22; Acts 1:8).

Our mission today is the same mission as that of the early church—to be witnesses of Jesus Christ and advance the new order of the kingdom Jesus established in the power of the Holy Spirit. The Christian witness must be more than the testimony of our lips. It must be the witness of a changed heart and life. We are first called to righteousness and holy living. The closer our walk is connected with our witness, the more of Jesus we witness to and the more believable our testimony. The Christ revealed to us must be formed in us by the Holy Spirit. Our witness must also be one that shares in the concern of Jesus for the needs of the poor, the oppressed, and those bound by the effects of sin in their lives. We must not polarize "activists" and "evangelicals," separating those who only want to "save souls" from those who want to feed the hungry, clothe the naked, and reform the oppressive structures of society. The world would see Jesus, but not a Jesus without skin on. When the Holy Spirit shapes our witness, there will not be one without the other.

Finally, our witness must be that of the proclaimed truth. Some reference to the Holy Spirit is either made directly or implied in every statement of the Great Commission (Matt. 28:18-20; Mark 16:15, 20; Luke 24:46-49; Acts 1:8). The Holy Spirit is the repeatable reality of Pentecost through which the gospel of Christ is proclaimed to the world.

LIFE APPLICATION
The Irony of Power

The irony of power is that, while power is essential to the gospel's success, it is the one thing that most easily corrupts. A desire for spiritual power apart from the Cross inevitably brings corruption and carnality. Paul knew the spiritual danger of knowing Christ "in the power of His resurrection" without a willingness to identify with Him "in His suffering" (see Phil. 3:10). One cannot claim the authority of Jesus and the power of the Spirit unless he or she is willing to identify with the Cross and accept its judgment on all forms of human power and wisdom. Any person that cannot emulate the crucified power of the Cross cannot be trusted with power. Jesus refused to exercise power in any way that was not in keeping with His calling, and through His example condemned forever the abuse of power.

Power was a particular concern for the New Testament church because it had been born and commissioned in power (Acts 1:8). The resurrection of Jesus and the sending of the Holy Spirit at Pentecost made the church aware of the newly released power in which they were living and carrying out their mission. But the experience of power also contained a spiritual threat. The Spirit-filled community had to be most careful at the point of its spiritual success. The Spirit richly gifted the Corinthian Church, but their abuse of power and spiritual gifts threatened the life of the congregation. The apostle Paul preached the gospel in power with many signs and wonders, but Paul also suffered much (Acts 9:16). The Cross was, for Paul, the power to triumph over cheap grace, rejoice in prison, suffer great deprivation, and count everything as loss for the surpassing worth of knowing Jesus as Lord.

Some today preach a gospel of health, wealth, and prosperity. Christians, they believe, can have as much as they have faith to name and claim. This point of view is far from the truth. It is not the purpose of faith to manipulate God and His will. Cross-bearing will always be an inevitable reality for those who live at cross purposes with this world. The person with extraordinary talent and personality struggles with the temptation to misuse it. They must guard against the tendency to win by force-of-talent and personality what ought to be won by force-of-character and goodwill. Jesus had to deal with this kind of temptation in the wilderness.

Jesus did not deny power; He redeemed it. He showed us its purpose—what God meant His power to be used for in our lives and ministries. *Power* is a word that is almost synonymous with *Pentecost*. For that reason, it is important that Spirit-filled Christians know its meaning and purpose. Our witness to Jesus is strongest when we allow the Spirit's power to be exercised in us as it was in Jesus. In a "me-ism" time, where selfish and easy success formulas abound, we must learn the meaning of crucified power.

DISCUSSION

The Spirit and Jesus
1. From the Gospels, give and discuss some examples of the joint mission and ministry of the Son and the Spirit.
2. Explain how the resurrection of Jesus refutes the idea of adoptionism.

The Holy Spirit in the Message of Jesus
1. What does the work of the Holy Spirit tell about the nature of the kingdom of God?
2. Why do you think the apostle Paul, in Romans 8:9, calls the Holy Spirit "the Spirit of Christ"?
3. In His parting discourse (John 14—16), Jesus referred to the Holy Spirit as the *paraclete*. Explain what Jesus was teaching His disciples in reference to the Paraclete (the Holy Spirit).

GLOSSARY OF TERMS/CONCEPTS

Adoptionism: The erroneous view, held by some in the early church, that God adopted Jesus of Nazareth and gifted Him with the Spirit so that He could fulfill God's purpose among the Jews. The error in this view is that it denies Jesus' eternal relationship with the Father (i.e., Jesus' divinity).

Blaspheming the Holy Spirit: This unforgivable sin is utter rebellion against God that denies the power of the Spirit and attributes it to evil forces hostile to God and humankind; a denial and rejection of the only power that can save (see Matt. 12:22-37). It is not a sin of ignorance but a willful rejection of the Spirit's work in Jesus Christ and the refusal to repent.

Irenaeus: An early church father (AD 130-200) who wrote against the Gnostic heresy and proposed the doctrine of *recapitulation*; that is, that Christ came to "sum up" and live out all that humans were meant to be in light of the sin of the first man Adam (see Rom. 5).

Kingdom of God: The central message of Jesus about the reign of God being inaugurated in the power of the Holy Spirit. It is a present reality in that Christ reigns now in the life of true believers. It is a future reality in that the Church awaits the future consummation of this age and the establishment of God's kingdom on earth during the Millennium.

Parting Discourse: The long passage, from John 13:31 through 16:33, that constitutes Jesus' farewell address to His disciples. Jesus was preparing His disciples for His departure and shared important truths with them, especially concerning the work of the Holy Spirit.

RESOURCES FOR ADDITIONAL STUDY

Horton, Stanley. *What the Bible Says About the Holy Spirit*. Springfield, Mo.: Gospel Publishing, 1976.

Lodahl, Michael. *The Story of God*. Kansas City: Beacon Hill, 1994.

McGrath, Alister. *Christian Theology*. Oxford: Blackburn, 1994.

Pinnock, Charles H. *Flame of Love: A Theology of the Holy Spirit*. Downers Grove, Ill.: InterVarsity, 1996.

Stronstad, Roger. *The Charismatic Theology of St. Luke*. Peabody, Mass.: Hendrickson, 1984.

Lesson 5

Living in the Spirit

For the apostle Paul, the Christian life is all about "living in the Spirit." From the first moment of the Christian life, the believer is living in the Spirit. The redemption accomplished through Christ's life, death, and resurrection is applied to the believer through the agency of the Holy Spirit. This re-creating and life-transforming reality changes us from what we once were in sin to a new creation in Jesus Christ.

In this lesson we focus on the working of the Spirit in different aspects of the believer's redemption, culminating in the work of the Spirit in sanctification. God's eternal plan of salvation (*soteriology*) looked forward to a covenant of grace that centered in the redemptive work of Christ and the appropriation of that work through the Holy Spirit. Following the basic outline of the order of salvation, drawn primarily from the apostle Paul, we will consider the following topics: (1) The new covenant in Christ; (2) The work of the Spirit in sanctification; and (3) The Holy Spirit as earnest and seal of the believer.

I. **THE NEW COVENANT IN CHRIST**
(Rom. 8:29-30; Gal. 3:2; Eph. 2:8-9; John 16:8; 2 Cor. 5:21; Rom. 5:1; Eph. 4:24; 2 Peter 1:4; John 3:3-8; Titus 3:5; Rom. 8:9; 1 Cor. 6:19; John 7:37-39; 14:20; 6:53; 1 Cor. 6:17; Rom. 8:15, 23; 9:4; Gal. 4:5; Eph. 1:5; Mark 14:36)

A. The *ordo salutis*, or order of salvation, described in the New Testament (Rom. 8:29-30) begins with the believer's *justification* before God. Justification is not based on human merit but on God's free grace responded to by the "hearing of faith" (Gal. 3:2 KJV; Eph. 2:8-9). The Spirit draws us into this relationship with Christ through the conviction of sin, a conviction that normally comes through the preaching and teaching of the gospel (John 16:8). In justification God accepts the sinner into His favor, offers him the forgiveness of sins, and imputes His righteousness to him (2 Cor. 5:21). The result is that we (saved from sin) are restored to God's favor, receive the peace of God, and are made free from condemnation through our Lord Jesus Christ (Rom. 5:1).

B. When the believer receives Christ by faith, the power of sin is broken and God imparts divine life to the soul. The believer, Paul says, is created anew after "true righteousness and holiness" (Eph. 4:24). The believer becomes a new creation in Christ Jesus and receives a new nature (2 Peter 1:4). This impartation of divine life and the receiving of a new heart is what we know as *regeneration*, a work made possible through the agency of the Holy Spirit (John 3:3-8; Titus 3:5). In *Redemption Accomplished and Applied*, Don Bowdle makes an important point regarding the work of the Holy Spirit in the order of salvation: "It is urgent to maintain here that every Christian possesses the Holy Spirit in regenerating measure. 'Now if any man have not the Spirit of Christ,' Paul says, 'he is none of his' (Rom. 8:9 KJV; see also 1 Cor. 6:19)." This does not mean every Christian is baptized with the Holy Spirit in regeneration. *Indwelling* and *infilling* are two different experiences. Without the former, one cannot be a child of God; without the latter, he cannot be fully effective in Christian witness and service (see John 7:37-39). It should be added that the focus of the apostle Paul is on the work of the Spirit in the order of salvation, not on the work of the Holy Spirit in Spirit-baptism, which pertains to Christian witness and service.

C. The work of the Spirit makes us His, not only in name but through a vital *union with Christ* that makes us His children (by *adoption*). Through this spiritual union, the believer participates in Christ. He indwells us and we are "in" Him (John 14:20). We are partakers of Christ (6:53) and one spirit with the Lord (1 Cor. 6:17). Because of our vital union with Christ, God has placed us in the position of adopted sons and daughters (Rom. 8:15, 23; 9:4; Gal. 4:5; Eph. 1:5). The Spirit indwelling us makes us conscious of our sonship and gives us confidence to greet the Father as Christ does (Mark 14:36).

II. THE JOURNEY OF SANCTIFICATION
(1 John 1:8-10; Rom. 6:1; John 17:17; Heb. 12:10; Rom. 12:1-2; Gal. 2:20; Col. 3:5-17; also read Rom. 6—8; Gal. 5:19-25; 6:8)

A. The new birth does not free the believer from temptation or the possibility of sin. Both Scripture and human experience teach the possibility, even the inevitability, that the believer will sin. Believers may think and behave in carnal and sinful ways. The apostle John wrote to Christians: "If we claim to be without sin, we deceive ourselves and the truth is not in us" (1 John 1:8). When we sin, John says, we are to confess our sin, receive God's forgiveness, and allow the blood of Christ to cleanse us from our sin (v. 9). As Christians we do not live in sinless perfection, but we are not to presume upon the grace of God. Paul asked the Romans, "Shall we go on sinning so that grace may increase?" (Rom. 6:1). His answer was, of course, a resounding "no." A Christian may commit sin, but the Christian's life is not characterized by sinning. Christians do not live under the dominion of sin. We have a new identity in Christ and a new power in us that is greater than the power of sin. Scripture is clear that God wills His people to be a holy people, cleansed by the blood of Christ and set aside for God's holy purpose. This is the essential meaning of *sanctification* (John 17:17; Heb. 12:10).

B. As Christians, we are called to pursue the new life that has been imparted to us through Christ. This entails holiness of heart and conduct. The goal of *sanctification* is Christlikeness, a reality made possible only through the power and presence of the Holy Spirit in our lives. We are to desire and submit to the purifying power of the Spirit in body, soul, and spirit. God is holy. Israel was called by God to be a holy people, and we are called by God to separation from sin and separation to God and His service. Things (e.g., the priest's garments) can be sanctified; days (e.g., the Sabbath) can be sanctified; but of more importance, persons can be consecrated to God and His service (Rom. 12:1-2).

C. There are two dimensions to our sanctification: *positional* and *practical*. *Positional sanctification* is the new relationship we have with Christ in justification and regeneration. The result of this work is death to sin and receiving the new life of our resurrected Lord (Gal. 2:20). As long as we keep our trust in the redemptive work of Jesus Christ, we are "positionally" holy in Him. *Practical sanctification*, on the other hand, is the ongoing pursuit of holiness of heart and conduct. The great challenge of the Christian life is to become in motive and conduct what we are already (positionally) in Christ. That is, to love God with all our heart, soul, mind, and strength, and to love our neighbor as ourself. As Christians, we have to continually deal with the pull and conflict we experience from the flesh (the carnal nature). The power of sin has been broken in the Christian's life, but we live continually in the presence of sin and its allurement. As Paul admonished the Colossians, there are attitudes and behaviors we must continually "put off" and those we must "put on" (Col. 3:5-17).

D. In Romans 6—8, Paul analyzes the ongoing spiritual conflict of the believer and identifies the means of victory we have in Jesus Christ through the power of the Holy Spirit. He first emphasizes that victory over sin requires believers to know their new identity. We identify fully with Jesus Christ through death and resurrection, symbolized in water baptism. Paul asks, "How shall we who died to sin live any longer in it?" (6:2 NKJV). We now have a new life, a new nature, a new Master. We live under the authority of a new kingdom and a new power. In Christ, we are not what we once were. It is therefore out of character for a true Christian to habitually sin (vv. 1-7). Victorious Christian living requires us to settle in our hearts and minds that we are "dead to sin," and we are "alive to God" (v. 11). There must be a continual dying of self to sin in order that we might know the life of the resurrected Christ. We return to the Cross time and again to submit our affections and desires to Christ (vv. 6-7). The journey of sanctification will end when we are finally glorified in our resurrected state, but until that time we continually struggle with the temptations of the flesh. Paul refers to the power of sin under many names: our old man, the body of sin, the sin that dwells in us, the law of our members, and the deeds of the body. The point is that sin, through its affections and lusts, continually seeks to have its way in our lives. Sin wants to rule, to have dominion over us (vv. 12-14).

Victorious Christian living requires that we, through the power of the Spirit, continually deny the rule or dominion of sin over our lives. We have forsaken the old life; we are now servants of God. We are submitted to the lordship of Jesus Christ and the standard of the Holy Spirit in our lives. Living according to the holiness and righteousness of Jesus Christ is the new norm for our life. This entails the continual yielding of the members of our body as "instruments of righteousness" (v. 13). This has implications for what we listen to, what we say, what we see, where we go, how we behave—involving our thoughts, desires, emotions, and motives.

In Romans 7, Paul graphically describes the struggle against sin that goes on in our thoughts, emotions, and will. Though we continually struggle against sin, our identity is not that of a sinner. Sin is not the dominant power in our life; it is an alien power. We belong to Christ and His kingdom. The source of victory, Paul says in chapter 8, is the "Spirit of life" in Christ Jesus (vv. 1-2). Our lives can be lived in one of two ways: "according to the flesh" or "according to the Spirit" (see

vv. 1-11). The indwelling Spirit of God is the life-giving power in the believer's life (Gal. 5:25). Living "according to the Spirit" and living "according to the flesh" have their natural outcomes. One leads to life, the other to death; one leads to the "fruit of the Spirit," the other to "works of the flesh" (see Rom. 8:5-11; Gal. 5:19-25).

The Holy Spirit produces a new kind of life and lifestyle in the believer—a life adorned by love, joy, peace, patience, kindness, goodness, faithfulness, gentleness, and self-control. This is the fruit of the Spirit (Gal. 5:22-23). Those who live according to the flesh do not belong to Christ and will not reap everlasting life (6:8). They yield to the things of the flesh, refuse to submit to God, and live in hostility toward God. Their works are according to the flesh: "adultery, fornication, uncleanness, lasciviousness, idolatry, witchcraft, hatred, variance, emulations, wrath, strife, seditions, heresies, envyings, murders, drunkenness, revellings, and such like" (5:19-21 KJV).

In Romans 8, Paul focuses on four works of the Spirit within the believer and the created order. First, he emphasizes that the Holy Spirit gives us our identity as children of God and assurance of our eternal inheritance (vv. 12-17). Second, despite the suffering and disappointment of this present time, the Spirit is leading His creation to future glory. The Holy Spirit has a new order, a new creation in store for those who love and serve the Lord. This is our future hope (vv. 18-25). Third, the Spirit helps us with our present infirmities by helping us pray according to the will of God. The Spirit cares for us and intercedes for us with groanings too deep for words (vv. 26-30). Finally, Paul encourages us to remember that in all situations God is for us. Nothing can separate us from His love and care. Our security is in Him. The Spirit communicates and assures us of the everlasting love of God (vv. 31-39).

III. THE HOLY SPIRIT AS EARNEST AND SEAL OF THE BELIEVER (2 Cor. 1:22; 5:5; Eph. 1:13-14; 4:30)

A. In several instances, Paul alludes to the indwelling Holy Spirit as the believer's "earnest" (KJV) and seal (2 Cor. 1:22; 5:5; Eph. 1:14). The Greek word for *earnest* is *arrabon*, a word frequently used in ancient contracts and agreements to refer to an advance payment, a first installment, or a pledge one makes to insure that in due time full payment will be made. Paul uses this term to say that the life we have now in the Holy Spirit is but a foretaste, a present guarantee, of the fullness of the Spirit we shall know in the age to come. The life and power of the future already abides in us now, but in due time we shall know that life and power in its fullness. From a moral and ethical perspective, we are to live now as though we were already living in our heavenly future. The life and power of the kingdom of God already manifests itself in the joy, peace, love, and righteousness we have in Christ through the Spirit.

B. The indwelling Spirit, Paul adds, has placed His *seal* upon believers, guaranteeing that we belong to Him (2 Cor. 1:22; Eph. 1:13; 4:30). When a document or goods were sealed in ancient times, the seal served as a guarantee or warranty that the sealer stood by and guaranteed the conditions and content of what had been said or sold. Paul uses the figure of the seal to say that the Holy Spirit is proof of God's faithfulness to His promises and His work. What the Spirit has begun, the Spirit will complete. God does not have spiritual orphans, nor does He leave His work unfinished. Our future is as sure as Jesus' resurrection from the dead and the indwelling presence of the Spirit. The seal of the Spirit continually reminds us that when Christ appears, we shall know Him in His fullness.

LIFE APPLICATION

The subject of sanctification has been, for many, controversial and misunderstood. Many actually shy away from the words *sanctification* and *holiness* because they feel these words represent more than they can live up to. It scares them because they are well aware of their failures and spiritual weakness. This should not be the case. Sanctification is not about how strong we are, but how strong the grace of God and the power of the Spirit are within us. Sanctification works from the inside out, not from the outside in. It is not about our holiness, but the holiness of Jesus Christ. It is not about our strength, but the power of the Spirit that indwells us. The purpose of sanctification is not to make us superhuman or anything other than normal "born-again" believers. The Spirit seeks to shape our motives and desires so that His graces can flow unhindered in us. As this happens, through the ongoing work of the Word and the Spirit, Christian growth will become obvious in our lives. While none of us will be perfect in this life, we do not have to live under the dominion of sin. This is not God's will for our lives. The completion of our sanctification will take place when we have come into complete conformity to Christ in our resurrected state (glorification).

Jesus is our example of the sanctified life. When Jesus ate with sinners, He showed that our primary concern is not sanctimonious behavior but loving others. Holiness of life is something positive; its purpose is not to establish moral superiority or enhance our spiritual status among fellow Christians. It is not a holier-than-thou way of life, but a wholehearted commitment to the way of Jesus Christ. In his book on *Christian Perfection*, John Wesley described Christian perfection as loving God with all our heart, mind, soul, and strength. He spoke of perfection not in terms of being a "perfect person" but in terms of pure motives and desires that have been perfected in love. As Christians, committed to holiness of life, we should always seek to become in life and conduct what we already are positionally in Jesus Christ.

DISCUSSION

The New Covenant in Christ
Explain why our conversion to Christ anticipates a holy life.

The Journey of Sanctification
1. Explain the difference between "sinless perfection" and "living under the dominion of sin."
2. Reading Romans 6—8, identify specific exhortations Paul gives for living victoriously over sin.
3. Describe the difference between the "fruit of the Spirit" and the "works of the flesh."
4. Can you explain the difference between positional and practical sanctification?

The Holy Spirit as Earnest and Seal of the Believer
Explain what Paul means by the "earnest" and "seal" of the Holy Spirit.

GLOSSARY OF TERMS/CONCEPTS

Christian Perfection: This term does not imply sinless perfection or infallibility on the part of the Christian. Rather, it means wholeness, maturity, and completeness in Christ. The sanctified life is wholly dependent on the grace of God and the agency of the Word and Spirit.

Earnest of the Spirit: The Holy Spirit dwelling in us as the *guarantee* that an even greater life with Christ will come in the future.

Justification: God's declaration that one's spiritual state is in harmony with the demands of the law of God.

New Covenant: A bond between God and man based on the inward righteousness of the heart, made possible through the life and death of Jesus Christ. The old covenant, by contrast, was between God and His people Israel. This covenant was based on Israel's imperfect righteousness prescribed by the laws and sacrifices in the Old Testament.

Ordo Salutis: The order or economy of God's eternal plan of salvation.

Positional and Practical Sanctification: *Positional sanctification* is the believer's new relationship to God following justification and regeneration. *Practical sanctification* is the pursuit of the renewal of the whole person after the image of God so that one can live unto righteousness and true holiness. Some hold that sanctification is a distinct experience of grace that purges the sin nature (Wesleyan emphasis). Others view sanctification more in terms of the ongoing conflict with the old nature, following the pattern of dying to self and living unto righteousness (Reformed emphasis). However, one does not necessarily exclude the other. What is most important is a strong theological and practical commitment to the transformed life and a love that obeys God.

Regeneration: The spiritual rebirth that takes place in the believer at conversion. Through regeneration, the believer becomes God's new creation with a new heart, or a new nature.

Sanctification: The main idea in sanctification is separation from what is sinful and consecration to God in righteousness and holiness. It is a work of divine grace in the believer subsequent to the cleansing work of Christ. The agents of sanctification are the Word and the Spirit.

Seal of the Spirit: The Holy Spirit dwelling in us as the official seal of God's ownership, marking the believer as His property.

Soteriology: From two Greek words, *soteria* (salvation) and *logos* (discourse). Soteriology deals with the provision of salvation through Christ and the application of salvation through the Holy Spirit.

Union with Christ and Adoption: A spiritual union with Christ through the Holy Spirit by which God accepts one as an adopted son or daughter.

RESOURCES FOR ADDITIONAL STUDY

Arrington, French L. *Christian Doctrine: A Pentecostal Perspective*. Vol. II. Cleveland, Tenn.: Pathway, 1992. 229-251.

Bowdle, Donald N. *Redemption Accomplished and Applied*. Cleveland, Tenn.: Pathway, 1972. 91-106.

Gause, Hollis. *Living in the Spirit: The Way of Salvation*. Cleveland, Tenn.: Pathway, 1980.

Lodahl, Michael. *The Story of God*. Kansas City: Beacon Hill, 1994. 25-30.

Wesley, John. *A Plain Account of Christian Perfection*. London: Epworth, 1979.

Lesson 6

Spiritual Gifting in the Church

In his correspondence with the Corinthian Church, known for its carnality and spiritual excesses, the apostle Paul gave much-needed instruction regarding spiritual gifts. In 1 Corinthians 12—14, Ephesians 4, and Romans 12, Paul expounded on this subject. The New Testament clearly teaches the importance of the gifts of the Spirit and admonishes us to not be ignorant of the Spirit's operation in the church. Yet, many are ignorant of the gifts of the Spirit, uninformed about the purpose of these gifts, and do not realize these gifts are for believers today.

In this lesson we focus on four topics: (1) the church at Corinth; (2) the purpose of spiritual gifts; (3) the operation of spiritual gifts in worship; and (4) a biblical model for true spiritual worship. Gifts come from the Holy Spirit and are distributed to the church as the Spirit wills. Their purpose is to glorify God and edify the church. They are not for one's private use but for the good of others. The diversity of gifts in the body of believers work for the completeness and unity of the church.

I. THE CHURCH AT CORINTH

A. The apostle Paul had founded the church at Corinth on his second missionary journey, probably around AD 50-52, and later corresponded with this church as its spiritual father. From all we know about this church, it had many practical and doctrinal problems. The problems in the church reflected the paganism and sensuality that existed in the city.

Corinth was a city in Greece governed by Rome. It was a port city strategically located to facilitate trade and commerce flowing in virtually all directions. It was known for its flourishing wealth and lustful pleasures, a sailor's town where everything seemed to be given to excess. Paul undoubtedly hoped that from this strategic city the gospel could be carried to the farthest regions of the world.

The morals of Corinth, however, were so low that the term *Corinthianize* had been coined to refer to people led into licentious excesses. The worldly habits of paganism that existed in Corinth had invaded the church. Fornication had crept into the church. There were factions. An erroneous doctrine had spread that the kingdom of God had fully come. Abuses of Christian freedom abounded. And, there was a selfish and loveless exercising of spiritual gifts. As James Moffatt noted in his *Commentary on 1 Corinthians*, "The Church was in the world, as it had to be, but the world was in the Church, as it ought not to be."

B. Paul's purpose in his correspondence to the Corinthians was to restore divine order in the church. This meant that instruction had to be directed to a number of issues, including the operation of spiritual gifts. As French Arrington emphasizes in his book, *Divine Order in the Church*, it was imperative that the church at Corinth follow the divine order of things in their worship and in the operation of the gifts of the Spirit.

II. THE PURPOSE OF SPIRITUAL GIFTS
(1 Cor. 12; Eph. 4; Rom. 12)

A. It is important, first, to be clear about the meaning and purpose of spiritual gifts. *Spiritual gifts* are divine enablements, given according to God's grace, for use in the body of Christ. God works in the church, through the gifts, to inspire and equip God's people for worship, ministry, and leadership. These gifts are available to all Christian believers, according to the will of the Holy Spirit, in order that the gifts might glorify God and edify the church. The church of our Lord Jesus Christ was not meant to operate in human weakness but in the power and presence of the Holy Spirit.

B Paul uses various terminology to describe spiritual gifts, calling them "gifts of grace" (from the Greek *charis*, from which we get the word *charismata*, which means "grace"), "spiritual gifts," and "manifestations of the Spirit." Paul means the same thing by these terms and uses them interchangeably. He emphasizes to the Corinthians that there are varieties of gifts, ministries, and operations of the Holy Spirit, but it is the same Spirit, the same Lord, at work in all of them (1 Cor. 12:4-6). Spiritual gifts have a variety of purposes and manifestations, but the same Spirit is working through all the gifts to glorify God and edify the church.

C. Gifts or operations of the Spirit should not be confused with natural gifts or talents. One may be born with natural talents, or develop

Spiritual Gifting in the Church

special abilities through learning and discipline, but spiritual gifts have their source in God's grace, given specifically for the edification of the church. This does not minimize natural and acquired abilities. The Spirit works to sharpen and use all of our abilities, if they are dedicated to Him.

III. THE OPERATION OF SPIRITUAL GIFTS IN WORSHIP
(1 Cor. 12—14)

A. Spiritual gifts operate through individuals, but they are not given for private or selfish purposes. They are for the common good of the body of Christ. Believers do not possess or control these gifts; they belong to God who gives them and are to be used as the Spirit wills (vv. 7-11). Paul emphasizes, however, that we should desire spiritual gifts, and welcome whatever way the Spirit wills to work in and through us (12:31; 14:1). Focus should not be on the gift, or the one through whom the gift is manifested, but on the Spirit's purpose to build up the church.

B. We need to know, however, that not all Christian duties and responsibilities depend on spiritual gifts. There are responsibilities all Christians share regardless of their gift(s). One may not, for example, have a spiritual gift for intercession, but all Christians have the responsibility to pray. One may not have a spiritual gift for evangelism, but this does not excuse them from being a witness of Christ. There are Christian responsibilities we all share, irrespective of the special working of the Spirit through His gifts.

C. In 1 Corinthians 12:8-10, Paul mentions nine gifts of the Spirit (wisdom, knowledge, faith, healing, miracles, prophecy, discerning of spirits, tongues, interpretation of tongues). This list should not be construed to mean, however, that there are only nine gifts. In other New Testament passages, some of these gifts are repeated and others are added (Rom. 12; Eph. 4). Paul was not attempting to give an exhaustive list of spiritual gifts, but was concerned to show that a diversity of spiritual gifts is needed for the varied needs and ministries of the church to be met. Christ, through the Holy Spirit, has gifted His church with all that is necessary for its life and mission. The Lord of the church has not set His church up for failure but for success. There are gifts for leadership in ministry (apostles, prophets, evangelists, pastor-teachers, administration); gifts for instruction (wisdom, knowledge); gifts for inspired speech (prophesying, discernment of spirits, tongues, interpretation of tongues); gifts of power (faith, healings, miracles); and gifts for practical service (giving, helps, service, mercy, exhortations). The church has been endowed by the Spirit for completeness and unity in the body of Christ. The completeness of the Body depends on all the members exercising the gifts God has given them. If they do so, the needs of the church will be met and God will be honored. The unity of the Body depends on every member's loving and selfless consideration of others in the exercise of his or her gift. Love must govern the exercise of all spiritual gifts (1 Cor. 13).

The church at Corinth was Pentecostal, but it was lacking in love. Paul opens chapter 14 by exhorting the Corinthians to "follow the way of love" (v. 1). This is the "more excellent way" (12:31). Speaking in tongues was a gift from God, but some had exalted this gift above others and created confusion in the worship. The gift of tongues, unlike the evidential/devotional tongue that accompanies the baptism in the Holy Spirit, is intended for use in public worship when accompanied by interpretation. Therefore, Paul says, the gift of tongues must be accompanied by interpretation so that the church can understand what God is saying and be edified. The aim of the gifts is to edify the church, not to "bless" the one exercising a gift. The Corinthians were abusing the purpose of spiritual gifts and carrying out their worship in a selfish and loveless manner. The one who speaks in tongues in a worship setting, Paul reminded them, is master of his own spirit and must show deference for others by maintaining control over the gift that is being exercised (14:32).

D. Prophesying too was subject to regulation. Paul instructed the Corinthians that no more than two or three prophets were to speak, and only one at a time. Others were to consider carefully what was said and discern whether or not the prophets' utterances were from God. No message was to be given uncritical acceptance. Every "alleged manifestation" of the Spirit is not the work of the Holy Spirit. Spirits must be tested to determine if they are from God, because many false prophets have gone out into the world (1 John 4:1; 1 Thess. 5:20-21). The test of what purports to be a spiritual manifestation from God is the Word of God. Critical questions must be asked: Is this manifestation consistent with the Word of God? Does it exalt the lordship of Jesus Christ? Does it promote the true gospel? Does it edify the church and glorify God? These are the ultimate tests of all alleged manifestations of the Spirit.

IV. A BIBLICAL MODEL FOR TRUE SPIRITUAL WORSHIP
(1 Cor. 13; 2 Cor. 3:17; 1 Cor. 14:40; 2 Cor. 4:7; 1 Tim. 4:11-16; Acts 13:1-3)

A. Paul's instruction to the Corinthians regarding spiritual gifts is particularly helpful in understanding the nature of true spiritual worship. Key principles can be discerned from the Corinthian correspondence. First, it should be noted that spiritual gifts are essential to the life of the church, its worship, and its mission. The ministry of the Holy Spirit can never be fully appreciated in a cognitive and intellectual manner alone. There must be a genuine openness to the Holy Spirit as an experienced reality. The church Jesus Christ founded is meant to be fully accepting of the operation of the Holy Spirit. The church is meant to be a community of faith in which the Spirit of God is recognizably present in power. The church is to be identified by its message—centered in the life, death, and resurrection of Jesus Christ—and it is also to be identified by its life in the Spirit.

B. Second, there must be freedom in the church for the Spirit to move as He wills. The operation of spiritual gifts, exercised under biblical principles, saves the church from formalism and deadness. A church that is too rigid and tightly structured with regard to the moving of the Spirit will inevitably experience a lack of life and power. "Where the Spirit of the Lord is," Paul wrote, "there is freedom" (2 Cor. 3:17). On the other hand, Paul admonished, freedom must always be exercised unselfishly with order and decency (1 Cor. 14:40). The church was meant to function in ordered liberty. Love is the key to ordered liberty. The exercise of the gifts with love is the "more excellent way" (12:31), which Paul refers to in chapter 13. All ministries and gifts are to be exercised through love—a self-giving love devoted to the edification of others.

C. Third, in the body of Christ there is a democracy of the Spirit in the sense that there is a place for every believer's gift. To be sure, God has called and gifted some for places of special leadership in the church, but lay members have a vital place of service in the church as well as those who have ministry gifts (Eph. 4:11-13). All Christians are equipped for service. All gifts consecrated to God's service and the edifying of the church are important to God. It is wrong to assume that less spectacular gifts are less spiritual or less important than more spectacular gifts. There are many ministries of the Spirit, but it is the same Spirit at work in all of them.

D. Finally, gifts are not a badge of spiritual superiority or maturity. The exercise of a spiritual gift does not necessarily mean God approves that person, his or her teachings, or behavior. The criterion of all that is taught and practiced is the Word of God. The fruit of the Spirit, not the exercise of a gift, reveals the Christian character of a believer. Paul reminded the Corinthians that spiritual gifts are "treasures [contained] in jars of clay" (2 Cor. 4:7). It is not our moral or spiritual superiority that determines how God distributes His gifts. Gifts are manifestations of God's grace at work. Spiritual gifts should encourage humility and a servant spirit in the congregation of the Lord. The fact that God chooses to work through weak human instruments requires the church to give spiritual oversight to its ministries and worship. Attitudes and behaviors that are carnal and do not edify the Body must be judged and corrected (see 1 Cor. 14:29).

E. The New Testament places a premium on balanced Christians and balanced churches. The balancing principle is evident in Paul's instruction to Timothy to neglect neither the prophetic gift nor the reading of Scripture. He was admonished to guard his manner of life and continue in sound doctrine (1 Tim. 4:11-16). In a similar manner, Luke described the church at Antioch as a balanced congregation of prophets and teachers who ministered in a community of sincere worshipers (given to prayer and fasting). The result was a spiritually sensitive church that sent out Paul and Barnabas to do the missionary work to which the Holy Spirit had called them (Acts 13:1-3).

LIFE APPLICATION

Pentecostal theologian Robert Menzies, in *Spirit and Power*, tells of a boyhood experience that many in the Pentecostal tradition can relate to: "I remember as a young boy attending a series of evangelistic meetings held in my hometown. The meetings were dynamic and inevitably included extended times of prayer at the altar. A number of people made public professions of faith, and there were many reports of healing. Several weeks after the meeting ended, we received word that the evangelist, who apparently had been so mightily used by God, had been living an immoral life. This news disturbed me and raised numerous questions.

Were the spiritual gifts I had witnessed genuine? Had God used this man to touch others in spite of his own weakness? I asked my father what he thought, and I still remember his response, 'Spiritual gifts are not necessarily given to those who are spiritually mature.'"

From this insight of his father, Menzies says he learned two significant implications for the life of the church. First, spiritual gifts are not necessarily linked to spiritual maturity, therefore we must not be awed by spectacular displays of spiritual power. Giftedness is not necessary related to spiritual depth, nor is it the criterion for spiritual leadership. Second, God sometimes bestows His gifts on those who are far from perfect. This should help us better understand that God can use us, as he did the Corinthians, despite our weaknesses. Gifts of the Spirit are not gifts based on merit, but gifts of grace. In this light, Paul did not admonish the spiritually elite to desire spiritual gifts but assured the church at Corinth that God delights to lavish His gifts of grace on all believers (1 Cor. 14:1).

DISCUSSION

The Church at Corinth
1. Describe comparisons you find between the church at Corinth and churches you know, particularly with regard to spiritual gifts.
2. Discuss Moffatt's statement: "The Church was in the world, as it had to be, but the world was in the Church, as it ought not to be."

The Purpose of Spiritual Gifts
1. Explain the meaning and purpose of spiritual gifts.
2. Why did Paul encourage the Corinthians to "desire" spiritual gifts even though there was an abuse of the gifts in the church?

The Operation of Spiritual Gifts in Worship
1. Explain the difference between the "gift of tongues" and "devotional tongues" which those who are Spirit-baptized may speak for personal edification.
2. Explain how Paul exhorted the Corinthians to regulate speaking in tongues in public worship. What does he say about prophesying?
3. How do you react to the statement that spiritual gifting is not necessarily an indication of spiritual maturity?

A Biblical Model for True Spiritual Worship
1. Describe what, in your view, a balanced church would look like today.
2. Describe the "most excellent way" Paul refers to in 1 Corinthians 12:31—14:1.

GLOSSARY OF TERMS/CONCEPTS

Charismata: Refers to God's grace bestowed in the form of some gift or gifts. The giver of the gifts (i.e., *pneumatica*) is the Holy Spirit.

Corinthianize: A term coined in reference to the debauchery and licentious excesses in the city of Corinth.

Gift of Tongues: This gift is for the edification of the church and requires interpretation when used in public worship. Paul indicates that God does not bestow this gift on all believers (1 Cor. 12:30).

"Most Excellent Way": Paul describes the "most excellent way" (v. 31) as love working with the spiritual gifts (see 14:1).

Spiritual Gifts: Divine enablements or endowments of grace bestowed on Christian believers for the edification of the church.

RESOURCES FOR ADDITIONAL STUDY

Arrington, French L. *Divine Order in the Church*. Cleveland, Tenn.: Pathway, 1978.

Barrett, C. K. *The First Epistle to the Corinthians*. Philadelphia: Westminster, 1956.

Conn, Charles W. *A Balanced Church*. Cleveland, Tenn: Pathway, 1975.

Cullmann, Oscar. *The Early Church*. Translated by A. J. B. Higgins and Stanley Godman. Philadelphia: Westminster, 1966.

Menzies, William W., and Robert P. *Spirit and Power: Foundations of Pentecostal Experience*. Grand Rapids: Zondervan, 2000.

Moffatt, James. *Commentary on 1 Corinthians*. London: Holder and Stoughton, 1938.

Spittler, Russell P. *The Corinthian Correspondence*. Springfield, Mo.: Gospel Publishing, 1976.

Lesson 7

Baptism in the Holy Spirit

Despite the attempts of some to marginalize the Pentecostal doctrine of the baptism in the Holy Spirit, this doctrine remains the unifying center of Pentecostal theology. It is therefore imperative that we understand the meaning and significance of this doctrine as traditional Pentecostals have understood it. To do this, we will focus on the *pneumatology* of Luke (Luke-Acts) that emphasizes the experience of the baptism in the Spirit and the prophetic dimension of the Spirit's activity. The three topics under consideration are as follows: (1) toward a definitive understanding of the baptism in the Spirit; (2) how the experience of the baptism in the Holy Spirit is received and maintained as a spiritual state; and (3) signs and evidences of the baptism in the Spirit.

Comparisons between the pneumatology in Paul's writings and in Luke-Acts will be drawn. Also, the relationship between the baptism in the Spirit and spiritual gifts, as well as the connection between the baptism in the Holy Spirit and Christian maturity, will be explored. The Pentecostal belief in speaking with tongues as the initial evidence of the baptism in the Spirit will be addressed. These and other topics make this a vital lesson for those in the Pentecostal and Charismatic traditions.

I. **TOWARD A DEFINITIVE PENTECOSTAL UNDERSTANDING OF THE BAPTISM IN THE SPIRIT**
(Matt. 3:11; Mark 1:8; Luke 3:16; John 1:33; Acts 1:5; 11:16; Luke 11:13; 24:49; Acts 2:33, 38-39; 8—11; 19; 1 Cor. 12:8-11; 14:1)

A. Although all Pentecostals do not believe and teach the same things about the baptism in the Spirit, there is a common body of teaching and experience among traditional Pentecostals that unify them in the doctrine of the baptism in the Holy Spirit. These common beliefs embrace the following three convictions: (1) Baptism in the Spirit is more than a doctrine, a sacrament, or a ritual act. It is an experience with God, through a distinct work of the Holy Spirit, that empowers one for Christian witness and service. (2) This experience does not result from special merit or spiritual maturity on the part of the recipient. Baptism in the Spirit is an eschatological gift, received in fulfillment of God's promise to make His people a prophetic community for the purpose of fulfilling the Christian mission. (3) Baptism in the Spirit should not be confused with conversion or sanctification. All aspects of life in the Spirit are, as the apostle Paul emphasizes, the work of the same Spirit, but the baptism in the Spirit is a distinctive work of the Holy Spirit. In this sense, it is subsequent to (i.e., it follows) conversion.

B. The first clarification that needs to be made is one of terminology. The word *baptize*, from the Greek verb *baptizo* (or its variants), is used six times in the New Testament with reference to the baptism in the Spirit. In each instance, baptism in the Holy Spirit is contrasted with John's baptism in water (Matt. 3:11; Mark 1:8; Luke 3:16; John 1:33; Acts 1:5; 11:16). It is worthy of note that every Gospel writer refers to this promise of the baptism in the Spirit. John the Baptist said, "I baptize you with water for repentance. But . . . he [Jesus] will baptize you with the Holy Spirit and with fire" (Matt. 3:11). After the 120 were filled with the Holy Spirit on the Day of Pentecost and spoke in tongues, the church knew they had received the baptism in the Spirit that Jesus had promised. This is made clear in Acts 11:16, when Peter declared, after the Holy Spirit had been poured out on Cornelius and his household, "Then I remembered the word of the Lord, how He said, 'John indeed baptized with water, but you shall be baptized with the Holy Spirit'" (NKJV).

C. Paul's treatment of the Spirit is a more developed perspective than that found in Luke-Acts, combining elements of the soteriological and charismatic dimensions of the Spirit's work. However, Paul and Luke both contribute to a harmonious understanding of the Holy Spirit that together present a full-orbed view of the Spirit's work. Though different, the two views are fully compatible, just as the four Gospels present a beautiful harmony of Christ and His work through their diversified accounts. The richness of Scripture is seen in the diversity that brings together and complements the whole.

D. The pattern that unfolds in Luke-Acts focuses on Jesus, the bearer of the Holy Spirit, who baptizes His disciples with the Holy Spirit to empower them for witness and service. As noted, John the Baptist prophesied that Jesus would baptize His followers in the Holy Spirit (Luke 3:16). Jesus reiterated the promise by assuring His disciples the Spirit would be given to those who ask the Father (11:13). The promise was again given to the disciples when Jesus commanded them to wait in Jerusalem until they were clothed with power from on high (24:49). The element of promise is also emphasized in Acts 1:5 and 11:16. In Peter's sermon on the Day of Pentecost, he referred to Jesus as the bearer of the Holy Spirit, who bestows the gift of the Spirit on His disciples: "Therefore having been exalted to the right hand of God, and having received from the Father the promise of the Holy Spirit, He [Jesus] has poured forth this which you both see and hear" (Acts 2:33 NASB).

The Old Testament prophet Joel (2:28) prophesied that in the last days the Spirit would be poured out on "all people"; that is, on Gentiles as well as Jews, without regard for age, gender, or social status. The pouring out of the Holy Spirit was the promised eschatological gift. It would not be restricted with regard to persons, place, or time. There would be no cessation of the Spirit or the Spirit's gifts. It would be a repeatable experience for the church until the coming of Christ. At Pentecost, Peter proclaimed that what happened to the 120 believers in the Upper Room in Jerusalem is promised to all who repent and turn to Jesus (Acts 2:38-39).

What happened in Jerusalem later happened in Samaria, to Saul of Tarsus, to Cornelius the Gentile and his household, and to believers in Ephesus. In Acts 8, Luke records that believers in Samaria were converted to Christ through the preaching of Philip the evangelist. Before they received the baptism in the Spirit, they had "believed" on Jesus (v. 12); they had "accepted the word of God" (v. 14); and they had been "baptized in water" (v. 12). This example clearly shows that the receiving of the Holy Spirit by the believers in Samaria was not a delayed climax to conversion as some have suggested (e.g., James Dunn and Gordon Fee). Rather, it was an experience subsequent to their conversion. It is instructive to note that Luke regularly separates the baptism in the Spirit from the rite of baptism in water that generally signifies conversion (e.g., Acts 2:4; 8:15-16; 9:17-18; 10:44-45).

Acts 9 tells about Saul of Tarsus receiving the Holy Spirit after his conversion on the road to Damascus. After Saul entered the city, God sent Ananias to him, that Saul might receive his sight and be "filled with the Holy Spirit" (v. 17). In connection with Paul's reception of the Holy Spirit, Luke emphasizes Paul's calling to the Gentiles (a prophetic emphasis). From the Book of Acts and Paul's letters to the churches he founded, we know the Spirit's prophetic anointing on Paul made his ministry effective in Asia and Europe.

Acts 10 tells about a Gentile named Cornelius, a man who feared God, gave liberally to the needy, and prayed much. When Peter preached the gospel to Cornelius and his household, the Holy Spirit fell on all who heard the Word. Jewish Christians who had accompanied Peter to Cornelius's house, though surprised at what happened, could not doubt that the Holy Spirit had been poured out on the Gentiles, because they heard them speak with tongues and praise God, just as they had done on the Day of Pentecost (vv. 44-48). Though this experience of their baptism in the Spirit was a distinctive work of the Spirit, it may well have happened in conjunction with their conversion, for they were subsequently baptized in water. What the Jewish believers had not expected was that God was calling Gentiles, as well as Jews, into the Christian mission. The church would soon learn that the Holy Spirit is impartial and inclusive toward all who receive Christ and desire to be His witnesses. Throughout the Book of Acts, the Holy Spirit is represented as working to break down man-made prejudices that separate people from God and each other.

Acts 19 gives the account of the twelve Ephesian disciples who had received John's baptism of repentance but had not heard about the Holy Spirit. On hearing this, Paul laid his hands on them and they received the Holy Spirit and spoke in tongues.

E. Pentecostals have rightly advocated the baptism in the Holy Spirit as being distinct from and subsequent to conversion (Acts 1:5, 8; 2:4), as well as the present reality of spiritual gifts in the church (1 Cor. 12:8-10). However, it is important to note there are other issues that have received less attention but are crucial to the overall understanding of the ministry of the Holy Spirit. One is the relationship between the baptism in the Spirit and spiritual gifts. Another is the relationship between the baptism in the Spirit and Christian maturity.

Early Pentecostal writers held a so-called "gateway position," arguing that the baptism in the Spirit is a door or gateway to spiritual gifts. However, in *Spirit and Power*, Pentecostal theologian Robert Menzies concludes: "While it cannot be maintained that Spirit baptism is the 'gateway' to every spiritual gift, the biblical evidence suggests that Spirit baptism is the 'gateway' to a special cluster of gifts described by Paul, the prophetic-type gifts that are associated with special revelation and inspired speech. Certainly it is true that, in one sense, every Christian is and should be increasingly charismatic. Paul highlights this fact: Every believer has something to contribute; everyone is enabled by the Spirit to contribute to the common good (1 Cor. 12:11). Yet it is also true that there is a dimension of the Spirit's enabling that one enters by virtue of a baptism in the Spirit distinct from conversion. This dimension might be properly called the prophetic dimension. In Luke's perspective, the community of faith is potentially a community of prophets; and it is by reception of the Pentecostal gift [baptism in the Spirit] that this potential is realized." Luke hoped this would become a reality in the church of his day (Luke 3:16; 11:13; Acts 2:17-18) as did the apostle Paul, who challenged the Corinthians: "Follow the way of love and eagerly desire spiritual gifts, especially the gift of prophecy" (1 Cor. 14:1).

The other issue of concern is the relationship between the baptism in the Spirit and the fruit of the Spirit, or Christian maturity. The Corinthian Church had no shortage of spiritual power, but many of them had carnal and sinful lifestyles. The confusion of spiritual power with Christian maturity oftentimes brings disappointment with Christian leaders deemed to be superior Christians because of their powerful ministries. But those who possess spiritual power may be lacking in Christian maturity and evidences of spiritual fruit. There should be a link between the prophetic and ethical dimensions of the Spirit in the life of every Christian, but this may not be the case. The Spirit of Pentecost is the Spirit of mission, the prophetic dimension in the believer's life. The Spirit as a soteriological agent, on the other hand, is the source of ethical transformation—the source of the fruit of the Spirit, holiness, and Christian maturity. The work of the Spirit was never meant to be bifurcated in our lives. Purity and prophetic power belong together. But as was evident in the Corinthian Church, and as is evident in the lives of some Christians today, this is not always the case. When it is not, the witness and the character of the church suffer loss.

II. HOW THE BAPTISM IN THE HOLY SPIRIT IS RECEIVED AND MAINTAINED AS A SPIRITUAL STATE
(John 14:16-17; Acts 5:32; Luke 24:45-49; Acts 1:8; Luke 11:5-13)

A. Baptism in the Spirit is a crisis experience. It is also a continuing spiritual state of being "filled with the Spirit" (Eph. 5:18). What is essential to the experience is also essential to the ongoing spiritual state. Baptism in the Holy Spirit is a promised gift, not something that can be received on the basis of works or merit. Understanding this, we can rightly talk about conditions for receiving the Spirit in terms of a right relationship or posture toward God that facilitates the receiving of His gifts and promises.

As Hollis Gause notes in *Living in the Spirit*, baptism in the Spirit is not an experience received through emotional conditioning, prescribed practices of worship, a legalistic lifestyle, or behavioristic manipulation. Some have labeled such emotional conditions and practices as the "moving of the Spirit" and have tried to establish unscriptural patterns of manipulated behavior as a necessary basis for the baptism in the Spirit. We must first understand that the Holy Spirit is "holy" and "personal." Consequently, one must enter into an interpersonal relationship with the Holy Spirit and submit to the Holy Spirit's character and purpose. The Spirit dwells in a holy temple, a temple that has been cleansed by the blood of Christ. Baptism in the Holy Spirit is not promised to the world, but to obedient believers (John 14:16-17; Acts 5:32). Baptism in the Holy Spirit is directly related to the mission of the Holy Spirit to bear witness to Jesus Christ (Luke 24:45-49; Acts 1:8). Apart from a commitment to a holy life, to more effectively serve God and others, and to bear witness to Jesus Christ, there is no point in seeking the baptism in the Holy Spirit. The experience of the baptism in the Spirit and the ongoing state of being "filled with the Spirit" presumes these standards.

B. Assuming that these conditions exist, candidates for the baptism in the Spirit should know it is the Father's good pleasure to give the gift of the Holy Spirit to those who ask Him (Luke 11:5-13). Yieldedness—self-surrender—is still the condition of the heart and mind the Spirit of God honors. Charismatic theologian J. Rodman Williams, comments on this point: "There exists a beautiful harmony between God's free action in the Spirit and our openness to it. The Spirit is a gift and therefore cannot be bought: consequently, there is no earning of the Spirit by any amount of prayers, vigils, and the like. The Spirit moves freely and cannot be compelled or coerced by any human contrivance—no matter how astutely performed. But for the very reason that the Spirit acts graciously in freedom, He will not grant a gift where it is not wanted or asked for, nor will He break through barriers that resist His coming. Thus only the open and expectant, the eager and hungry, the askers and seekers (not because of what they do but because of their readiness) receive God's blessings" (*The Era of the Spirit*, p. 62).

Under what conditions should believers expect the coming of the Holy Spirit? Hollis Gause answers that question from a scriptural perspective: "We can expect the coming of the Holy Spirit when the body of Christ meets in one mind and one accord. We can expect the outpouring of the Holy Spirit where believers join together in praising and blessing God. . . . We can expect the gift of the Spirit to be bestowed while the Word is being preached. We can expect the baptism [in] the Holy Spirit to be given when hands are laid on fellow believers in obedience and faith . . . He delights to give His Spirit to those who ask Him (Luke 11:9-13). In all of our seeking we must place greater affection on the Giver of the experience than upon the experience" (*Living in the Spirit*, p. 85).

III. SIGNS AND EVIDENCES OF THE BAPTISM IN THE SPIRIT
(Acts 2:4; 10:44-48; 19:1-7; 1 Cor. 14:18-22)

A. One of the most often asked questions concerning the baptism in the Holy Spirit is whether or not "speaking in tongues as the Spirit gives the utterance" is the "initial physical evidence of the baptism in the Holy Spirit." This is a legitimate question, and one that deserves an answer, especially in light of the fact that many have cast doubt on this long-held Pentecostal conviction. It is important, on one hand, to understand the nature of the relationship between tongues (*glossolalia*) and the baptism in the Spirit and, on the other hand, not to erroneously equate the Pentecostal gift with tongues. Let us first clarify that the believer does not seek for an experience of tongues. The sign or evidence of the baptism in the Spirit is important, in that it points to the purpose of the Holy Spirit, but it must not be understood as the purpose itself.

The strength of the Pentecostal argument for tongues as the "initial evidence" is the purpose Luke-Acts gives for the baptism in the Spirit—namely, prophetic witness. Throughout Luke-Acts, the Pentecostal gift is directly linked to inspired speech. When one receives the gift of the Holy Spirit, it is only natural that the Spirit manifests His presence and power in inspired speech. Luke's emphasis on the gift of the Spirit is focused on the Spirit as power for effective witness. In light of this prophetic emphasis, there should be no surprise that inspired speech, or speaking in tongues as the Holy Spirit gives the utterance, is the physical sign of this experience.

B. Some who reject evidential tongues as a normative doctrine do so because they say one cannot establish that Luke, in the Book of Acts, "intended" to teach evidential tongues. There is no "proof text" for the doctrine, nor is the pattern that unfolds in Acts uniform (e.g., Gordon Fee). Consequently, these critics say, Pentecostals have no right to insist on evidential tongues. Pentecostals, however, see three examples in Acts that point to a definite relationship between being filled with the Spirit and speaking in tongues. The first is at Pentecost itself, which constitutes the normative experience: "And they were all filled with the Holy Spirit, and they began to speak with other tongues because [*kathos*: because] the Spirit was giving them inspiration to speak" (2:4, translation of Hollis Gause). Luke's language clearly indicates a causative relationship. The Holy Spirit's presence was manifested by Spirit-inspired speech.

The second example, with the same causal relationship, is reflected in the pouring out of the Holy Spirit on Cornelius and his household (10:44-46). Peter, and the Jews who accompanied him, were convinced these Gentiles received the gift of the Holy Spirit, because they heard them speak with tongues as they had at Pentecost: "And the believers out of the circumcision who accompanied Peter were amazed that even upon the Gentiles the gift of the Holy Spirit had been poured out, for they [i.e., because] were hearing them speaking with tongues and magnifying God" (vv. 45-46). Furthermore, the leadership in Jerusalem was satisfied the Gentiles had received the Holy Spirit because of the same correlation (11:15-18).

The third example is found among the believers in Ephesus: "When Paul placed his hands on them, the Holy Spirit came on them, and they spoke in tongues and prophesied" (19:6). From these instances, the correlation between the gift of Pentecost, speaking in tongues, and prophecy in the Book of Acts is undeniable.

C. Many have been confused by Paul's question to the Corinthians, "Do all speak in tongues?" (1 Cor. 12:30). The construction of this question implies a negative answer. With regard to tongues as the initial evidence of the baptism in the Spirit, however, this text is not an issue. Paul was referring to tongues as a spiritual gift, not as the initial physical evidence of baptism in the Spirit. The distinction that should be made is between what some describe as "devotional tongues" and the gift of tongues. Devotional tongues, which is proper for Spirit-baptized believers, edifies only the speaker and is intended for private rather than public worship. The gift of tongues, on the other hand, is given for public worship and demands interpretation so the church can be edified. Tongues (glossolalia) may communicate prayer and praise, but has a prophetic character that carries with it the message of God.

Devotional tongues is a sign that serves two purposes: It is a physical evidence of the experience of the baptism in the Spirit, and is also for personal edification. As a spiritual gift, tongues serve two functions as well: for communication and edification in the body of Christ (provided there is interpretation), and as a sign to unbelievers—as the strange tongues of foreigners were a sign of God's judgment on the disobedient nation of Israel (1 Cor. 14:21-22; cf. Isa. 28:11-12).

D. Finally, it should be noted that, while the Scriptures support the view that speaking with tongues as the Holy Spirit gives the utterance is the initial physical evidence of the baptism in the Spirit, this is not the only evidence of being filled with the Spirit. The surest sign of the Spirit-filled life is submission to Jesus Christ as one's Lord. Living a life of genuine love, and of obedience to the Word of God, are evidences that cannot be counterfeited. Speaking with tongues should never be taken as proof of one's holiness, maturity, or spiritual superiority. Tongues have a spiritual purpose that should not be minimized. Still, we must never become so awed by, or preoccupied with, any spiritual manifestation that we lose a balanced, biblical perspective on the Spirit-filled life.

LIFE APPLICATION

In *Azusa Street and Beyond*, Grant McClung characterizes the modern Pentecostal Movement as ecumenical, cross-cultural, and missionary in nature. He also notes that it could be regarded as a "student movement."

The movement actually began in Topeka, Kansas, in the Bible school operated by Charles Parham. Historian Vinson Synan describes what happened:

> By December 1900, Parham had led his students through a study of the major tenets of the Holiness Movement, including sanctification and divine healing. When they arrived at the second chapter of Acts, they studied the events which transpired on the Day of Pentecost in Jerusalem, including speaking with other tongues.

At that juncture, Parham had to leave the school for three days for a speaking engagement. Before leaving, he asked the students to study their Bibles in an effort to find the scriptural evidence for the reception of the baptism with the Holy Spirit. Upon returning, he asked the students to state the conclusion of their study, and to his "astonishment" they all answered unanimously that the evidence was "speaking with other tongues." This they deduced from the . . . recorded occasions in the Book of Acts when tongues accompanied the baptism with the Holy Spirit (Acts 2:4; 10:46; 19:6).

Apparently convinced that his conclusion was a proper interpretation of the Scriptures, Parham and his students conducted a watch-night service on December 31, 1900, which was to continue into the new year. In this service, a student named Agnes Ozman requested Parham to lay hands on her head and pray for her to be baptized with the Holy Ghost with the evidence of speaking in tongues. It was after midnight and the first day of the twentieth century when Miss Ozman began "speaking in the Chinese language" while a "halo seemed to surround her head and face."

Following this experience, Ozman was unable to speak in English for three days, and when she tried to communicate by writing, she invariably wrote in Chinese characters. This event is commonly regarded as the beginning of the modern Pentecostal Movement in America.

After Ozman experienced "tongues" the rest of the students sought and received the same experience. Somewhat later, Parham himself received the experience and began to preach it in all his services (Synan, The Holiness-Pentecostal Movement in the United States, pp. 101-102).

Shortly thereafter, a student at Parham's second school in Houston, Texas, received the Pentecostal experience and took the message of Pentecost to Los Angeles, California, where he began the famous Azusa Street Revival that lasted three years (1906-09). This African-American's name was William J. Seymour, and he became the spiritual father of the revival that launched the Pentecostal Movement throughout the world.

DISCUSSION

Toward a Definitive Pentecostal Understanding of the Baptism in the Spirit
1. What is the biblical basis for the terminology "baptism in the Holy Spirit"?
2. Explain the basic difference between pneumatology in Paul's writings and in Luke-Acts.
3. Give some explanation of the Pentecostal belief that the baptism in the Holy Spirit is subsequent to conversion.

How the Baptism in the Holy Spirit Is Received and Maintained as a Spiritual State
1. Describe what candidates for the baptism in the Spirit should do to receive the experience.

2. Explain the significance of the baptism in the Spirit as the promised Pentecostal gift.

Signs and Evidences of the Baptism in the Spirit
1. How does "tongues as initial evidence" fit naturally with the Luke-Acts account of the baptism in the Spirit?
2. How would you respond to critics who claim that Luke's account in Acts does not intend to teach tongues as the initial evidence of the baptism in the Spirit? (Reflect carefully on the following texts: Acts 2:4; 8:14-19; 9:17; 10:44-48; 19:1-7; 1 Cor. 14:18).

GLOSSARY OF TERMS/CONCEPTS

Baptism in the Holy Spirit: A distinctive Christian experience, subsequent to conversion, according to the pattern of Acts 2:4.

Cessationism: The view of some that miracles and the more extraordinary gifts of the Spirit were terminated at or near the end of the apostolic age.

Glossolalia: A Greek word meaning "to speak in tongues." It refers to the supernatural ability to speak in languages not previously learned, as happened on the Day of Pentecost (Acts 2:4).

Pneumatology: The doctrine of the Holy Spirit. From the Greek words *pneuma* (spirit) and *logos* (the teaching about).

Subsequence: The Pentecostal belief that the baptism in the Holy Spirit is distinct from and follows the experience of conversion.

RESOURCES FOR ADDITIONAL STUDY

Gause, Hollis. *Living in the Spirit*. Cleveland, Tenn.: Pathway, 1980.

Hunter, Harold. *Spirit Baptism: A Pentecostal Alternative*. Lanham, Md.: UP of America, 1980.

Macchia, Frank D. *Baptized in the Spirit: A Global Pentecostal Theology*. Grand Rapids: Zondervan, 2006.

Menzies, William W., and Robert P. *Spirit and Power: Foundations of Pentecostal Experience*. Grand Rapids: Zondervan, 2000.

Sims, John. *Power With Purpose*. Cleveland, Tenn.: Pathway, 1984.

Stronstad, Roger. *Charismatic Theology of St. Luke*. Peabody, Mass.: Hendrickson, 1984.

Lesson 8

The Holy Spirit and Eschatology

Eschatology is a theological term that comes from the Greek word *eschaton*, meaning "last things." Understanding the Pentecostal perspective on eschatology, or end-time events, is crucial to understanding what energizes and integrates the theology of Pentecostals. Pentecostal views on eschatology are not necessarily unique, but Pentecostals are unique in their view that the outpouring of the Holy Spirit is the eschatological gift sent to renew and empower the Church for its last-day witness. From the beginning of the movement, Pentecostals had strong expectations of the *imminent* return of Christ. They believed the outpouring of the Holy Spirit upon the Church in these last days was for the purpose of evangelizing the lost and preparing the Church for Christ's return.

Eschatology is not simply a "last word" in Pentecostal theology, a doctrine added to other doctrines; it is a passion that integrates what Pentecostals believe and how they live. This lesson will focus on three aspects of Pentecostal eschatology: (1) a Pentecostal perspective on end-time events; (2) eschatology and the experience of hope; and (3) the Spirit and new creation.

I. **A PENTECOSTAL PERSPECTIVE ON END-TIME EVENTS**
(Hos. 6:3; Joel 2:23-32; Zech. 10:1; Ezek. 37—39; Dan. 7—9; Matt. 24—25; Mark 13; Luke 21; 1 Thess. 4:13—5:11; 2 Thess. 2:3-12; Rev. 19—20; Mark 13:26; Luke 21:27; John 5:24; 2 Cor. 5:10; Rom. 14:10; Acts 17:31)

A. Pentecostals have always had an intense interest in eschatology. Some scholars even see the eschatological motif as the integrating core of the Pentecostal message (e.g., Robert Mapes Anderson, David William Faupel, and, to some extent, Donald Dayton and Steven Land). As we will note later, eschatology, for Pentecostals, is more than a series of future events; it is an experience of hope. Pentecostals are an eschatological people, filled with the eschatological gift (the Holy Spirit), living with expectation of the imminent return of Christ. This expectation gives Spirit-filled believers a sense of urgency as a prophetic community seeking to fulfill the end-time mission of preparing the church and the harvest for the second coming of Christ. The mission is to be accomplished, Pentecostals believe, in the power of the Spirit and the restored spiritual gifts in the body of Christ.

B. Pentecostal eschatology has always been linked to the imagery of the early and latter rain mentioned in the Old Testament. There were two major seasons of rainfall in Palestine (Hos. 6:3; Joel 2:23-32; Zech. 10:1). The first came in the fall and prepared the soil for planting. This "former rain" (KJV), Pentecostals believe, corresponded to the first Pentecost (Acts 2), which initiated the work of the church in planting the gospel seed.

In Palestine, the "latter rain" (KJV) occurred in the spring of the year. These rains ripened the crops for harvest. Pentecostals believe this corresponded to the great outpouring of the Holy Spirit in modern times for the purpose of renewing the church and preparing the world (the harvest) for the return of Christ. Gifts and miracles reappeared in an extraordinary manner because God was giving special signs of His presence and power, equipping the Church for its task.

The "last days" spoken of in the New Testament actually refer to the time between the ascension of Christ and His second coming, but certain end-time events such as the return of the Jews to their homeland were indications that the coming of Christ was near. These prophetic signs clearly energized Pentecostals to evangelize the world and prepare the church for the imminent return of Christ.

C. Jewish eschatological hopes centered in the prophetic literature of Daniel, Ezekiel, Zechariah, and other texts; but after the Babylonian Exile, Israel's hope for the future was closely linked to the nation's messianic hope (Isa.). In the New Testament, the end times became a major theme in the teachings of Jesus. Virtually all of the New Testament writers addressed the subject in some manner. Jesus spoke often of the future aspect of the kingdom of God in His parables. In the Gospels, whole chapters were given to the theme of end-time events (Matt. 24—25; Mark 13; Luke 21), and some New Testament books like 1 and 2 Thessalonians and Revelation are especially focused on the subject. In the apostolic and post-apostolic church, there was a clear expectation of the imminent return of Jesus Christ, and it is worthy of note that several church fathers held

The Holy Spirit and Eschatology

a premillennial view of Christ's return. Pentecostals have always held to a premillennial perspective regarding the return of Christ.

D. To put this aspect of Pentecostal eschatology in perspective, it is necessary to provide some historical background. Following the Civil War in America, the postmillennial vision of revivalist preachers like Jonathan Edwards and Charles Finney began to be seriously challenged by premillennial advocates. The turn to premillennialism by large numbers of religious leaders in America was due to a number of factors. Two reasons were particularly prominent: (1) a closer examination of the teachings of Scripture and (2) historical/cultural events that were seriously calling into question the optimism of the postmillennial vision. In actuality, events in the late nineteenth century (the ravages of war, a downturn in morality, Darwinian evolution, philosophical naturalism, and the "higher criticism" of the Bible) made it difficult for Bible-believing Christians to be optimistic about the establishment of an earthly kingdom of God brought by human progress. The clear teaching of Scripture and the events of the time made premillennial expectations much more realistic.

The strength of premillennialism, too, was that it did not spiritualize away the prophecies contained in the Book of Revelation, nor did it diminish the expectancy of Christ's return. The glory of the firstfruits of "last things" had already appeared in history with the resurrection of Jesus from the dead and the outpouring of the Holy Spirit at Pentecost, but Scripture clearly taught that the fullness of that glory would follow the second appearance of Christ (Mark 13:26; Luke 21:27).

E. The general outline of Pentecostal beliefs regarding "last things," following the return of Christ, tended to center around future judgments. The Scriptures teach that there are many judgments that will take place in the future. The most important judgment for the believer, however, has already taken place. Those who have believed in Jesus Christ, whose sins have been forgiven, have already had their sins judged at the Cross. They have been freed from the penalty and guilt of sin (John 5:24) and will not be judged in the future for sins that have been forgiven. Their appearance before the judgment seat of Christ will be to receive rewards (2 Cor. 5:10; Rom. 14:10).

Future judgments, on the other hand, include the judgment of Israel, referred to as "the time of Jacob's trouble" (Jer. 30:7 KJV), and graphically described in the Book of Revelation (chs. 13-17) as a period of great tribulation that shall come upon the whole world for seven years. The Scriptures speak of the judgment of Babylon, a world government or political power that supports the apostate spiritual power on the earth (17:1—19:5). Near the end of the Great Tribulation, the Antichrist (the Beast) and the False Prophet (the apostate spiritual leader) and their followers will be judged (19:19-21; 2 Thess. 2:8). Following this, the Scriptures tell that the nations will be gathered for judgment prior to the beginning of the Millennium (2 Thess. 1:7-10; Matt. 25:31-46; Joel 3:11-17; Acts 17:31). After this, the next thousand years, Christ will rule and reign on the earth.

At the end of the Millennium, Satan, the fallen angels, and all unclean spirits will be judged and cast into the "eternal fire prepared for the devil and his angels" (Matt. 25:41; see also Rev. 20:1-3, 7-10). The final judgment will be that of the unbelievers of all ages. This is a judgment of the unrighteous dead, both "great and small," who will stand before God at what is referred to as the "Great White Throne" for the judgment of their sins (Rev. 20:11-15). This judgment will take place at the end of the Millennium, just prior to the creation of the new heavens and the new earth (the eternal abode of the righteous).

F. Pentecostal eschatology had many things in common with *dispensationalism*, a view that gained wide acceptance among fundamentalist Christians around the turn of the twentieth century. This view was popularized, in part, through the notes contained in the Scofield Reference Bible. Pentecostal and dispensationalist views, however, were by no means identical. In some cases they were antithetical.

Both Pentecostals and dispensationalists read the Scriptures with a similar emphasis on future events, including a pre-Tribulation rapture of the Church. But Pentecostals found many dispensationalist views objectionable. Especially questionable is the view that God has dealt with the human race in different ways, other than grace, during different periods of human history. Most identify seven dispensations, or periods of time, when faith has been tested by specific revelations of God's will. Most troubling is the distinction between a dispensation of law and a gospel of grace.

Pentecostals take special offense at the dispensationalist view of the gifts of the Spirit and the nature of the Church. In the dispensationalist view, there is no real continuity between the people of God in the Old

… The Holy Spirit and Eschatology

Testament and New Testament. God's dealings with Israel are viewed as different from His dealings with the Church. Dispensationalists are quick to reject miracles and spiritual gifts in the present-day church. They believe they were temporarily present in the apostolic church, but that miracles and extraordinary gifts ceased when that age ended. This view, known as *cessationism*, is offensive to Pentecostals because it does not have the support of Scripture, church history, or experience. It only serves to discourage believers from expecting the supernatural operation of God's power and gifts in the church.

II. ESCHATOLOGY AND THE EXPERIENCE OF HOPE
(1 John 3:3; 1 Cor. 15:26, 54-56; Rev. 21:4; 1 Cor. 1:30; 1 Thess. 4:7; 2 Cor. 7:1; Rom. 8:23; 2 Cor. 5:5; Eph. 1:13-14; Book of James; Rom. 8:18-25)

A. Eschatology is more than a set of expectations regarding future events; it is a present spiritual reality. The Gospel of John beautifully emphasizes that eternal life does not simply mean the extension of life after death; eternal life is a different quality of life that has already been introduced by Christ and made available to believers through the indwelling Holy Spirit. As believers in Christ, we already experience the life and power of the Kingdom; we already have a taste of the life of the age to come.

Inherent in the Christian's hope, however, is an ethical and moral imperative. As believers in Christ, what we hope to become transforms what we are presently, for "everyone who has this hope in him purifies himself" (1 John 3:3). As Christians, we are not merely enduring this present life, we also await the great transforming events of the future. We are already enjoying a foretaste of the quality of life we will one day know in its fullness.

Life in the Spirit is to be lived now in accordance with the power and norm of the future. As long as we are in this world, we will live in the presence of sin, but the Holy Spirit wills to deliver us from sin's power. We will never reach Christian perfection in this life, but through God's grace and the indwelling presence of the Holy Spirit, we can live victorious Christian lives. Sin, suffering, and death will be finally abolished when Christ returns to complete the work of redemption (1 Cor. 15:26, 54-56; Rev.

21:4), but even now the new life we enjoy through the Spirit has begun to shape what we are in Christ.

The Holy Spirit, by His very nature, opposes sin and carnality. He seeks to shape our lives according to the holiness and righteousness to which we have been called (1 Cor. 1:30; 1 Thess. 4:7). He calls us to "purify ourselves from everything that contaminates body and spirit, perfecting holiness out of reverence for God" (2 Cor. 7:1). Those filled with the Spirit take the same posture toward the world the Spirit takes because of His holy nature and witness. God does not transport us out of the world when we become believers in Christ, nor does He call us to live in isolation from the world. Rather, He empowers us with the Holy Spirit to live in the world without living by its values, loyalties, and standards.

As believers, we have not yet experienced all we will experience in terms of re-creation. That must await the return of Christ and our glorification. But the indwelling Spirit foreshadows all that is yet to come (Rom. 8:23). The Holy Spirit is the *guarantee* (*arrabon*) of our future inheritance and is, also, an advance installment of it (2 Cor. 5:5; Eph. 1:13-14). The promise of God concerning our future is clear. What God has already begun in us by the power of the Spirit, He will complete at His coming. The resurrected Christ is the *firstfruits* (*aparche*) of the Christian's future glory.

B. Those who believe in the imminent return of Christ, whose premillennial eschatology teaches them that the end is near, are not called to live indifferently to the needs of this present world. Martin Luther believed that the second coming of Christ was near in his time (the sixteenth century); but he remarked that if he knew Christ were coming tomorrow, he would still plant his apple tree today. We are to occupy until He comes. Eschatological futurism must never obscure a Christian vision for a better world. Christian ministry is more than "snatching brands from the fire." Hope is a gift of the Spirit, but this hope is clothed in love and Christian responsibility toward others. This includes compassion, care, and social responsibility toward the poor, the marginalized, the oppressed, and those who suffer from the injustices of society.

Social concern was never meant to be something tacked on to the gospel for good measure, to somehow round it all out. Christian concern for human need and suffering is part of the gospel itself, as evidenced by the actions of the early church. Genuine concern for the needs of others and self-giving action toward them are the surest proofs of the gospel's power to penetrate and transform human life. Faith must be active in love (Book of James).

We err when we assign to the future what God has called us to participate in now. The fullness of the Kingdom has not yet come, but the Kingdom has broken through in the power of the Holy Spirit. Theologian Daniel Jenkins was right, I believe, when he stated: "The wilderness through which we pass must not be treated with indifference . . . we must claim as much of the world for the Kingdom as we can. We are colonists of heaven as well as a pilgrim people. We have a responsibility to refashion as much of the world as we can after the likeness of our homeland. We are a people 'called out' for others."

A church indwelt by the Holy Spirit will give witness in the world to the end toward which it is moving and the future which is coming to meet it. We should add, however, that Christians do not bear the burden of providing utopian answers to this world's problems. The fulfillment of history will come only from beyond history. God must be trusted to consummate what He has begun.

In the power of the Spirit we are to live faithfully and productively in the interim between the "already" and the "not yet." Life in the "already" dimension of the Spirit redeems us from paralysis and withdrawal from human need and suffering. The "not yet" dimension, on the other hand, saves us from too much optimism regarding the transformation of this present world. We know the consummation of God's kingdom will not come through growth in history. Christ must consummate and finalize that which He has already begun. Until that day, the Holy Spirit within us will not cease to groan and long for the day when all of creation will experience final redemption (Rom. 8:18-25).

III. THE SPIRIT AND NEW CREATION
(Eph. 4:7-10; 1 Cor. 15:28; Rev. 21:1-8; Rom. 5:5; 1 John 4:8; Eph. 3:17-18; Matt. 5:8)

- A. The ultimate goal of creation is for God's reign to be fully manifested throughout the created order. In that day, Paul says, the Spirit of God will fill all of creation (Eph. 4:7-10). When His kingdom comes in its fullness, God will be "all in all" (1 Cor. 15:28). Everything will be reordered to the glory of God. What we now know as a "foretaste" will be fully realized. Individual Christians being "filled with the Spirit" anticipate on a micro-level what will occur when all of creation becomes the temple of God's presence and power.

The goal of the kingdom of God is for all of creation to become the temple of God's presence. Already, the Holy Spirit indwells God's people and, in that day, He will indwell all of creation as God's presence filled the Temple. All of creation will be renewed, freed from imperfections, and transformed by the glory of God as the Almighty finally tabernacles with all of creation. In that day, there will be no more pain and sorrow. Life will reign over death. All things will be made new. God's dwelling will become our dwelling for eternity (Rev. 21:1-8).

B. Pentecostals are an eschatological people, passionate about the return of Christ. Why would we not be? In his landmark work, *Pentecostal Spirituality: A Passion for the Kingdom*, theologian Steven Land emphasizes that eschatology has been the impetus that drives the transformation of Pentecostal passions. He describes *sanctification* in terms of the transformation of the affections and passion for the coming fullness of the kingdom of God. Land sees the integration of purity and power, driven by the hope and passion for the Kingdom, as the most distinctive aspect of Pentecostal theology. It is the life-changing reality that marks Pentecostal experience, transforming what we are into what we shall become.

Love is the supreme gift God gives us at the beginning of our spiritual journey. The Holy Spirit pours this gift into our hearts (Rom. 5:5). Love is the essence and substance of the Trinitarian life, mediated between the Father and the Son by the Holy Spirit (1 John 4:8). It is this love that shapes our affections, our passions, and our commitment to the mission of Christ. What we know of this love now, however, is but a foretaste of what we shall one day know when we "[comprehend] with all the saints" and "grasp how wide and long and high and deep is the love of Christ" (Eph. 3:17-18).

Just as the triune God exists in the divine community of Father, Son, and Holy Spirit, the redeemed will one day live in a glorified community of saints. The people of God will exist as God does in a holy community of individuals, forever relating to God as holy sons and daughters, and to each other in holy love. The kingdom of God will have come in its fullness—not simply for a last generation, but for the redeemed of all ages. In the light of God's divine presence, we shall know Him and be free to love and serve Him, and one another, in ways that we can now hardly imagine. In the glory of that "new heaven and new earth" (Rev. 21:1), He will fill all things, and the promise of Jesus will finally be realized: "Blessed are the pure in heart, for they will see God" (Matt. 5:8).

LIFE APPLICATION

The doctrine of last things is the great hope of the Church; it is also a sobering subject that puts many things into perspective. It reminds us that our individual lives and the life of the universe as a whole are finite. The existence of all things, as we know them, will someday come to an end. All is creaturely—we are dust, subject to corruption and decay. All that we are and all that we do must be evaluated in light of the future that God has ordained.

Eschatology reminds us that we do not live a meaningless existence. God has a goal, a purpose, for His creation. The doctrine of last things allows us to understand that things will end according to His purpose. It assures us of God's authority over all things, of His sovereignty over nature and history. The end will verify that God's Word, inspired by the Holy Spirit, is indeed true. It assures us that righteousness will ultimately triumph over the powers of sin and evil. Everything will be brought to its end by God's providential leading, as we are taught in the Book of Revelation.

The doctrine of last things reminds us of human responsibility and divine judgment. The story is told of an eighteenth-century Jewish rabbi named Zushya. As Zushya lay on his deathbed, he lamented to those gathered around how little he had accomplished during his lifetime. One of his students asked the rabbi if he feared that divine judgment awaited him. He began to reply "yes," but stopped himself. "No," he said. "When I appear before the Almighty, I will not be asked, 'Why were you not Moses?' or 'Why were you not David?' I will only be asked, 'Why were you not Zushya?'"

God knows us for what we truly are. "Nothing in all creation is hidden from God's sight. Everything is uncovered and laid bare before the eyes of him to whom we must give account" (Heb. 4:13). He knows when we have chosen the lesser road. He knows what we have done with the gifts and graces He has given us in this life. He knows if we have been faithful and true. In one of His parables, Jesus reminded His hearers that much will be required of those to whom much has been given (Luke 12:48).

The beginning, the middle, and the end of the Christian story cannot be separated. The plot holds together in the unity of the whole. It is the beginning that discloses the purpose of the end. The end reveals the completion of the beginning. The middle, Jesus Christ, is the center and significance of the beginning and the end. "I am Alpha and Omega, the beginning and the ending, saith the Lord, which is, and which was, and which is to come, the Almighty" (Rev. 1:8 KJV).

DISCUSSION

A Pentecostal Perspective on End-Time Events
1. Read Revelation 19 and 20. Identify the order of end-time events mentioned in these chapters.
2. Explain the difference between a *premillennial* and a *postmillennial* expectation of the return of Christ.
3. What is *dispensationalism*? What disagreements do Pentecostals have with this interpretation of the Bible?

Eschatology and the Experience of Hope
1. What do we mean when we speak of the Christian experience of hope?
2. In light of the imminent return of Christ, what responsibility do Christians have for the social order of this present world?

The Spirit and New Creation
1. Read Revelation 21 and 22. Describe what is revealed in these chapters.
2. Explain how the doctrine of last things serves to integrate major teachings of Pentecostal doctrine.

GLOSSARY OF TERMS/CONCEPTS

Cessationism: The view that extraordinary gifts and miracles ended at or near the end of the apostolic era.

Dispensationalism: A system of theology, delineated in the notes of the Scofield Reference Bible, that suggests God has worked with people in different ways (dispensations) of history. God, in this view, has a distinct plan for Israel that is different from that of the Church. This view also advocates cessationism.

Eschatology: The theological study of the end of history, wherein Christ returns to earth to establish His eternal kingdom of righteousness and justice among all nations.

Imminent: A term that refers to the fact that the coming of Christ could occur at any moment. No established intervening events have to take place before His return, thus ruling out all predictions of the time or date of His coming.

Postmillennial: The view that Christ's second coming will follow the Millennium, and which anticipates a moral and spiritual influence by Christians that will prepare the earth for the coming of Christ.

Premillennial: The view that the return of Christ will precede the thousand-year reign of Christ on the earth with His saints.

RESOURCES FOR ADDITIONAL STUDY

Dayton, Donald W. *Theological Roots of Pentecostalism*. Grand Rapids: Zondervan, 1987.

Faupel, William. *The Everlasting Gospel: The Significance of Eschatology in the Development of Pentecostal Thought*. Sheffield, England: Sheffield Academic Press, 1996.

Hughes, Ray H. *Church of God Distinctives*. Cleveland, Tenn.: Pathway, 1968.

Land, Steven J. *Pentecostal Spirituality: A Passion for the Kingdom*. Sheffield, England: Sheffield Academic Press, 1993.

Macchia, Frank D. *Baptized in the Spirit: A Global Pentecostal Theology*. Grand Rapids: Zondervan, 2006.

Lesson 9

The Pentecostal Century

The outpouring of the Holy Spirit in the twentieth century resulted in the greatest revival in the history of the Christian church. In fulfillment of what Joel prophesied concerning the pouring out of the Holy Spirit on all flesh, the "latter rain" revival has brought millions of souls into the Kingdom and unprecedented renewal to the church. This lesson is more historical than preceding lessons, recounting in abbreviated form some of the highlights of the story of how God raised up, from humble beginnings, a worldwide movement that today constitutes the largest family of Protestants in the world. The Pentecostal and Charismatic renewal movements have reached across denominational barriers, restored spiritual gifts to the church, and transformed the life and worship of the Christian church.

Our narrative will, of necessity, be brief and focused on limited topics. These will include: (1) The origins of Pentecostalism; (2) Azusa Street and beyond; (3) the forming of Pentecostal denominations and missionary fervor; (4) the rise of the Charismatic Movement and the "third wavers."

I. THE ORIGINS OF PENTECOSTALISM

The origin of Pentecost goes back to the Day of Pentecost when the Holy Spirit was poured out on the 120 believers in the Upper Room in Jerusalem (Acts 2). Pentecost was a harvest celebration that followed the gathering of the wheat crop in Israel. It was a joyous feast filled with singing and dancing as the people rejoiced at the harvest bounty given by the Lord. This feast day had spiritual and prophetic significance for Israel; it also has great significance for the church in that the "early and latter rain" necessary for the harvest has to come before the return of the Lord (see James 5:7-8).

The church was empowered for its mission in the "early rain" outpouring that began on the Day of Pentecost. The "latter rain" outpouring was promised for the last days before the return of Christ. The church is living now in the "latter rain" stage of human history (Joel 2:28-29; Acts 2:16-21). Within one generation, following Pentecost, Christianity spread over the known world, but it has only been in the last century that the prophecy of Joel has been fulfilled in its fullest sense. In the late nineteenth and early twentieth centuries, a worldwide outpouring of the Holy Spirit occurred, accompanied by spiritual gifts. That Pentecostal rain is still reaping a harvest of souls and preparing the church for the soon return of Jesus Christ.

The outpouring of the Holy Spirit in the last days has been a sovereign move of God, but it has not been a rootless phenomenon. What is occurring today has its roots in the New Testament church. The church we read about in the New Testament was a church that lived in the Spirit and in which the spiritual gifts operated freely. After Constantine, when the church became more institutionalized and turned more to ritual and sacramental expressions of the faith, the church experienced less and less of the miraculous power and gifts of the Spirit. Attempts of renewal movements like the Montanists (AD 185-212) and the Jansenists (17th century) were stifled by the institutional church, but as Catholic theologians Kilian McDonnell and George Montague have documented through scholarly research, the ministry of the Holy Spirit continued. For centuries there were Christians who regarded baptism in the Spirit as an integral part of Christian experience, and their experience of the Spirit was accompanied by spiritual manifestations like those experienced at Pentecost (Acts 2).

In the mainstream of the Western church, however, such experiences were condemned after the promulgation of the "cessation theory" advocated by Augustine and John Chrysostom. The Rituale Romanorum (i.e., Roman Ritual), around AD 1000, went so far as to declare glossolalia evidence of demon possession. The Orthodox churches of the East never adopted the cessation theory; but during the Protestant Reformation, Luther and Calvin continued to perpetuate the cessationist perspective on spiritual gifts. In the Catholic tradition in the West, gifts and miraculous deeds were oftentimes attributed to the "saints" and the "mystics," but apart from less spectacular gifts like government, administration, and teaching reserved for the hierarchy of the church, the gifts of the Spirit were suppressed.

It was not until the nineteenth century that a significant number of Protestant churchmen began to expect a restoration of the gifts of the Spirit in the church. This interest was ignited by a renewed interest in Bible prophecy and the imminent return of Christ. Reports of miracles and the gifts of the Spirit were reported in Scotland and in London, England, where Edward Irving, pastor of the prestigious Presbyterian church on London's Regent Square, openly encouraged a restoration of the gifts in his church. Irving was passionate for a restoration of New Testament Christianity. Charles Spurgeon, the great Baptist preacher in London, and William Arthur, a Methodist preacher, spoke openly and enthusiastically of their expectation that a "New Pentecost" could happen at any time.

Phoebe Palmer, a well-known Methodist preacher and teacher, helped popularize talk about Pentecost in America. Asa Mahan, president of Oberlin College, also used the language of Pentecost. The roots of Pentecostal language, however, can be traced further back to John Wesley and his colleague John Fletcher, who spoke of "sanctification" and "baptism in the Holy Spirit" as essentially the same experience. In holiness circles, the term *Pentecostal* was frequently used in reference to sanctification through a baptism in the Holy Spirit. No real distinction was made among holiness folk between sanctification and baptism in the Spirit. Some "holiness" denominations even referred to themselves as Pentecostal churches (e.g., the Pentecostal Church of the Nazarene). Methodist and holiness believers, praying around the mourner's bench in holiness churches and camp meetings, sought a sanctifying experience of heart purity—an experience they believed could happen in an instant through a baptism in the Holy Spirit.

Pentecostal language was also rooted in the camp meeting tradition, especially after the Civil War. The great camp meetings began in 1801 in Cane Ridge, Kentucky, and spread quickly across America. After the disruption of these meetings by the Civil War, the camp meeting tradition was rebirthed with the organization of the "National Camp Meeting Association for the Promotion of Holiness" in Vineland, New Jersey, in 1867. Again, camp meetings sprang up across the nation, this time promoting the doctrine and experience of sanctification. Nineteenth-century spirituality in America centered in these highly charged camp meetings where seekers earnestly sought for the conversion and sanctification experiences. After 1867, the word *Pentecostal* was increasingly used to describe the post-conversion "second blessing" experience of sanctification.

Another development relating to sanctification was taking place in England and America during the last few decades of the nineteenth century. This was the emergence of the Keswick "Higher Life" conferences in England and the Northfield Conferences in Massachusetts conducted by the famous American preacher D. L. Moody. These conferences were a counterpart of the American National Holiness Association, but with a different understanding of sanctification. In contrast to those in the Wesleyan-Holiness tradition who emphasized sanctification as a "second blessing" experience that eradicates the sinful nature in the believer, the Keswick and Northfield emphasis held that sanctification is a baptism in the Holy Spirit that endues one with "power for Christian service." The Spirit-filled life was seen as an anointing of the Spirit for service more than an experience of cleansing. The Keswick emphasis moved away from sanctification as a "second work" or "state of Christian perfection" to an ongoing spiritual condition in the life of the believer that had to be spiritually maintained.

In America, D. L. Moody, R. A. Torrey, Adoniram Gordon, and A. D. Simpson were advocates of the Keswick perspective on the Spirit-filled life. These competing views on sanctification later erupted into an open controversy between the "finished-work" advocates (Keswick view) and the "Holiness" advocates who taught that sanctification is a "second work" of grace, subsequent to conversion, that eradicates the sin nature. Advocates of both views were convinced their view had the support of Scripture. Pentecostals today do not oppose one another as strongly as they once did over the doctrine of sanctification, but for some time it was a doctrine that was strongly contested.

Benjamin Irwin, founder of the Fire-Baptized Holiness Church, was an important bridge from the Holiness Movement to Pentecostalism in America. In 1895, Irwin experienced what he called a "baptism of fire" which he referred to as the "third blessing" (i.e., an experience subsequent to conversion and sanctification). It was in a Fire-Baptized holiness revival in the Shearer Schoolhouse, in the region bordering North Carolina and Tennessee, that the Holy Spirit was poured out on some holiness folk who spoke in tongues (1896). This was the first outpouring of the Holy Spirit on a small group of believers who would later become known as the Church of God (Cleveland, Tennessee).

The infilling of Agnes Ozman with the Holy Spirit, with the evidence of speaking in tongues, at Charles Parham's Bethel Bible School in Topeka, Kansas, provided the doctrinal basis for Pentecostal theology. After Ozman's experience, and the evidence he found for it in the Book of Acts, Parham openly taught that the baptism in the Holy Spirit, with the initial physical evidence of speaking in tongues, is a "third blessing" experience. Pentecostalism grew out of Methodism and the nineteenth-century

Holiness Movement, but their "third blessing" doctrine of baptism in the Spirit, with the evidence of tongues, set them apart from their holiness brethren. Holiness churches quickly rejected the doctrine of Pentecostals and disassociated themselves from the language of Pentecost.

It is important to note, however, that Pentecostals were not entirely focused on one experience or doctrine. As scholar Donald Dayton observed in his groundbreaking work, "Theological Roots of Pentecostalism," early Pentecostal doctrine centered in Jesus as Savior, Spirit baptizer, Healer, and coming King. Their doctrinal roots were synonymous with the great evangelical truths of the Bible.

II. AZUSA STREET AND BEYOND

William J. Seymour carried Charles Parham's message of a "third blessing" experience, accompanied by tongues, to Los Angeles, California. Seymour was a black preacher from Louisiana who had received his training at Parham's Bible school in Houston, Texas. For three years, Seymour led the famed revival at Azusa Street that ushered in the Pentecostal Movement.

Reports of the revival meeting first appeared in the *Los Angeles Times* on April 18, 1906, under the headline "Weird Babel of Tongues." It was not a new phenomenon. The same manifestations had occurred in Edward Irving's church in London, in camp meetings on the frontier, in the experience of D. L. Moody and Agnes Ozman, and in the Welsh revival of 1904. It was now, however, occurring daily in the revival meetings on Azusa Street. The revival in Wales, led by Evan Roberts, had seen over 30,000 converts and had ignited a worldwide hunger for revival in the churches. Holiness pastors in Los Angeles had been praying earnestly that a new Pentecost would come to their city. Frank Bartleman, a holiness minister, was so hungry for a "new Pentecost" that he published a tract titled "The Last Call," prophesying one last "worldwide revival" before the judgment of God. Bartleman closed his tract by predicting, "Some tremendous event is about to transpire."

What transpired on Azusa Street in the next three years was more than just another revival. Thousands from around the world came to the mission to witness a sovereign move of the Holy Spirit. Many were simply curious. Others were critical of what they regarded as mere emotional gibberish and fanatical physical manifestations in a run-down livery stable. Integrated ethnic groups and races from various parts of the world were engaged in strange behaviors and receiving an experience accompanied by languages they could not understand.

In meetings that often lasted throughout the night, Seymour walked through the crowds exhorting the people to "let the tongues come forth . . . ask for salvation, sanctification, the baptism with the Holy Ghost, or divine healing." Visitors claimed they could feel a supernatural atmosphere for blocks surrounding the mission. The services were punctuated by weeping, dancing in the Spirit, trances, and speaking and singing in tongues. Accounts of the meeting soon spread across the nation in both the secular and religious press. Bartleman and Seymour published papers that kept readers across the nation informed about what was happening on Azusa Street. Trains in Los Angeles daily unloaded passengers from all parts of America coming to witness and seek the blessings of the new Pentecost.

What began as a local revival led by an illiterate preacher from the South was soon drawing the attention of people from around the world. From the standpoint of doctrine, the important thing about the Azusa Street Revival was that it raised to doctrinal status the "third blessing" experience and evidential tongues. From a historical and practical perspective, the revival gave birth to a movement that rapidly spread around the globe.

III. THE FORMING OF PENTECOSTAL DENOMINATIONS AND MISSIONARY FERVOR

Leaders from various holiness denominations came to the mission, received the baptism in the Holy Spirit, and returned home to lead their churches into the Pentecostal ranks. One of these was Charles Mason, founder of the Church of God in Christ (based in Memphis, Tennessee). Bishop Mason played a vital role in the spreading of the movement and its message.

G. B. Cashwell from Dunn, North Carolina, came from the South as well, received his baptism in the Spirit, and returned home to spread the fires of Pentecost. The Church of God (Cleveland, Tennessee) and the Mountain Assembly Church of God (Kentucky) embraced the Pentecostal doctrine through the teaching and influence of Cashwell. This pattern was repeated throughout the United States. Florence Crawford took the message of Pentecost to Portland, Oregon. William Durham carried the torch of Pentecost to Chicago. Maria and Robert Brown took the message to New York City; Roswell Flower, to Indiana and the Midwest. A. H. Argue carried the Pentecostal message to Canada, where the movement spread rapidly.

The new movement was not confined to North America. T. B. Barratt, a Norwegian Methodist pastor, was visiting America in 1906 and heard about the outpouring of the Holy Spirit in Los Angeles. Barratt was convinced this was the "latter rain" outpouring of the Holy Spirit that he had been expecting. He planned to travel to Azusa Street to seek the Pentecostal blessing, but began praying for the experience in New York. Barratt received his baptism in the Spirit in New York and spoke and sang in other tongues. He returned to Oslo, Norway, where he rented a gymnasium seating two thousand and began the first recorded Pentecostal meeting in Europe. Barratt became the prophet and father of European Pentecostalism. Influential pastors from Sweden, England, and Germany attended Barratt's meeting, received the baptism in the Holy Spirit, and returned to their countries spreading the Pentecostal message. Lewi Pethrus from Sweden, Jonathan Paul from Germany, and Alexander Boddy from England were all brought into the movement through the influence of Barratt. Italian-Americans who received the experience spread the message to their relatives back in Italy, and that country was soon filled with Pentecostal churches. After World War II, the movement began to grow in France, Spain, and Portugal—largely through the ministry of the American evangelist T. L. Osborne. Through mass conversions in the Gypsy population in the 1950s, Pentecostalism spread rapidly across the European continent.

The latter rain that had fallen in America and Europe was falling in South America. William C. Hoover, a Methodist missionary in Chile, longed for a repetition of the things he read about in the Book of Acts. Through a vision given to a member of his congregation and the prayers of the church, a historic revival began in Hoover's congregation in Valparaiso that soon spread to Santiago, the nation's capital (1909). Thousands crowded into Hoover's church, where gifts of the Spirit were manifested and Spirit-filled believers danced in the Spirit. Every Sunday, members of the church preached on the streets of Valparaiso, following a slogan that is still used today by Chileans: *"Chile sera para Cristo"* ("Chile will be for Christ").

In 1910, Swedish immigrants Daniel Berg and Gunnar Vingren traveled from the United States to Brazil, where they founded the Assemblies of God (four years before the Assemblies were organized in America). They came in contact with Pentecostals in the Chicago area and responded to a prophecy instructing them to go to an unknown place called "Pará." They discovered from a world atlas that "Pará" was a region in Brazil. Through their faithfulness to the Lord, and God's miraculous provision, they were able to establish the largest Protestant community in Brazil.

The growth of Pentecostalism in Latin America has been phenomenal. It is not uncommon for Methodist, Baptist, and Presbyterian churches to add the name "Pentecostal" to their churches to attract larger crowds. Well over 50 percent of Protestants in Latin America are Pentecostals. Today, Pentecostals constitute the largest family of churches in Brazil, Argentina, Chile, Peru, Ecuador, Colombia, Panama, El Salvador, Honduras, and Mexico.

Ivan Voronaev, born in central Russia, was a Baptist pastor before immigrating to the United States in 1911. He received the baptism in the Holy Spirit in New York. Shortly thereafter, he returned to the Soviet Union after a prophetic utterance persuaded him to do so. Voronaev became known as the "Pentecostal Apostle to the Slavic Nations" but was eventually martyred in a communist prison.

Pentecostalism originated in India, apart from events in North America or Europe, validating the fact that the outpouring of the Holy Spirit was a worldwide phenomenon. Forty years before the Pentecostal revivals in Europe and America, Indian believers were praying for and receiving the outpouring of the Spirit with accompanying gifts of prophecy and tongues.

Minnie Abrams (1859-1912), a Methodist missionary, was a Pentecostal leader in India after the turn of the century. She operated a school for orphan girls where unusual manifestations of the Spirit took place. Abrams reported that, on one occasion, a young girl had been baptized in the Holy Spirit and "fire" (Matt. 3:11). She saw the "fire" and ran across the room for a pail of water. As she was about to pour the water on the young girl, she discovered the girl was not on fire. This "baptism of fire," Abrams believed, signified the purification of sanctification and urged confession of sin and repentance. Minnie Abrams wrote a popular work titled "Baptism of the Holy Ghost and Fire," urging believers to pray for the purifying power of the Holy Spirit. Abrams was an example of the many women who made great contributions to Pentecostal missions. It is worthy of note that, for many decades, women constituted the majority of Pentecostal missionaries.

The first Pentecostal missionaries to reach China in 1907 were T. J. McIntosh and his wife. The Garrs, who had served in India, followed them to China, as did Martin Ryan. A Pentecostal revival broke out among Alliance missionaries in China that transformed their ministries. Missionaries soon took the gospel as far as Tibet and, in 1922, Swedish Pentecostals ventured to Inner Mongolia. In 1908, Sisters Daniels and Brand from California took the gospel to Korea. In 1928, Mary Rumsey, who had received her baptism in the Spirit at Azusa Street, joined them. Life for missionaries in Asia was difficult. Many buried their spouses and children there, but their passion to be witnesses of Jesus Christ was stronger than the many hardships they endured. These early missionaries in Asia sowed some of the seeds that are producing so much fruit today in China, Korea, and Indonesia.

Pentecostalism entered Africa primarily through South Africa. Two early missionaries to South Africa who made a great impact were John G. Lake and Thomas Hezmalhatch. Lake served only four years in South Africa (1908-1912), but he established the two largest Pentecostal churches in the country. He was known as the "Apostle of Pentecost to South Africa." Advances followed into Liberia and Angola. Missionaries later entered Ghana and Nigeria. Eventually, the continent of Africa became one of the great success stories of missions.

Pentecostals were not without their problems, their excesses, or their schisms. Following the peak of the Azusa Street Revival, a major controversy erupted within the movement over the doctrine of sanctification. Most early Pentecostals came out of the Wesleyan-Holiness movement. In this tradition, sanctification was viewed as a second definite work of grace. As more Baptists entered the movement, a more reformed view of sanctification emerged known as the "Finished-Work" doctrine; or, as some called it, "Baptistic Pentecostalism." The leading advocate of this doctrine was William Durham, a Chicago pastor who began preaching the Finished-Work message in 1910. Finished-Work theology denied that a residue of sin remained in the believer after regeneration. We are entirely cleansed from sin through the work of the Cross. After conversion, the believer still wars against the "flesh," but not against a sin nature. The Finished-Work doctrine saw sanctification as an ongoing progressive work in the life of the believer, not as a second crisis experience. The baptism in the Holy Spirit, from the

Finished-Work perspective, was not a third experience but a work of the Spirit subsequent to conversion.

The Finished-Work doctrine spread quickly throughout the Midwest, particularly among ministers outside the influence of the Southern holiness movements. Many who were associated with groups who embraced this more progressive view of sanctification came together in Hot Springs, Arkansas, in 1914 and organized a fellowship of Pentecostal ministers known as the "Assemblies of God." Leaders in the organization of this movement were E. N. Bell, Howard Goss, Daniel Opperman, Archibald Collins, and M. M. Pinson. In time, the Assemblies of God became the fastest-growing Pentecostal denomination. Two things distinguished the Assemblies of God from the Wesleyan-Holiness Pentecostals. The first was a more progressive view of sanctification; the other was their congregational form of church polity. That is to say, the denomination was organized around autonomous local assemblies. Most other Pentecostal groups followed an episcopal form of church polity that had more centralized forms of church government. Theologically, The Assemblies of God were more in the Reformed tradition that had influenced the Keswick movement in England and the Oberlin theology in America.

Another controversy arose within the Assemblies of God, over the Trinitarian question, when the movement was still in its infancy. A group of ministers in the Assemblies, the "Oneness" advocates, contended that the Bible does not teach a Trinity. They ascribed the Trinitarian doctrine to the heretical teaching of Roman Catholics. They believed there is only one divine personality—Jesus Christ. All other designations, such as "Father" and "Holy Spirit," are mere titles. They taught that the only legitimate formula for water baptism is in "Jesus' name" (see Acts 2:38). They equated baptism in the Spirit with water in "Jesus' name," the evidence of which is speaking in tongues. Everything for the Oneness advocates was collapsed into the one experience of baptism in water in Jesus' name. Frank Ewart is generally regarded as the "father" of the Oneness movement. Many Oneness believers were in independent, nonaligned churches. But in 1945, a Oneness group was formed called The United Pentecostal Church. The unitarian "Jesus only" theology was rejected by virtually all Pentecostals. In later years, this group was refused membership in the Pentecostal Fellowship of North America.

There were controversies in other Pentecostal churches as well. In 1920, there was a controversy in the Pentecostal Holiness Church over the doctrine of divine healing that resulted in the organization of the

Congregational Holiness Church. Also, a scandal over the tithing system and what some considered the autocratic control of the general overseer, A. J. Tomlinson, resulted in a schism in the Church of God (Cleveland, Tennessee). Out of this controversy, a new church was formed named the Church of God of Prophecy.

Aimee Semple McPherson formed the last major Pentecostal denomination in 1923 in Los Angeles, California. This body is the International Church of the Foursquare Gospel—the "foursquare gospel" being salvation, baptism in the Spirit, divine healing, and the second coming of Christ. This group had an early association with the Assemblies of God and embraced the Finished-Work doctrine. Aimee Semple McPherson was a dramatic and charismatic figure. She built the vast Angelus Temple, the first Pentecostal megachurch, and became a celebrity in the Los Angeles area, drawing huge crowds to the services in the temple.

IV. THE CHARISMATIC RENEWAL AND THIRD WAVERS

Pentecostal historian Vinson Synan describes the early history of Pentecostals in society as one of mutual rejection. Pentecostals rejected society because they believed it to be corrupt, hostile, and hopelessly lost. Society rejected Pentecostals because they believed them to be fanatical, emotionally unstable, and erroneous in their doctrine. This did not change very much until midcentury when certain developments began to reshape attitudes toward the movement. Chief among these developments were the continued growth of the movement, the ascent of more and more Pentecostals into the middle class, the influence of divine-healing crusades (especially Oral Roberts), the Full Gospel Businessmen's Fellowship International, and David du Plessis, known as "Mr. Pentecost," who served as an ecumenical spokesman and catalyst for Pentecostals.

The most important ecclesiastical development occurred in 1942, when many Pentecostal churches were invited to join the National Association of Evangelicals (NAE). A few years later, The Pentecostal Fellowship of North America (PFNA) was formed for the purpose of promoting fellowship and unity among Pentecostals (1948). The worldwide growth and influence of Pentecostals so impressed Henry Van Dusen, president of Union Theological Seminary in New York, that he wrote an article in *Life* magazine in 1958 titled "The Third Force in Christendom." In this article, Van Dusen argued that a major force now existed in the Christian world alongside traditional Catholicism and Protestantism.

Van Dusen's insights were prophetic of what would soon happen to the face of Christianity in the latter half of the twentieth century through the Charismatic Renewal Movement.

David duPlessis, a South African Pentecostal leader, felt (as early as the 1930s) that God was going to bring renewal to the historic denominations. During the 1950s and 1960s, that expectation began to take place on a level few would have dared to expect. For years, those in the traditional churches who received the Pentecostal experience and spoke in tongues had only two options: they could either leave their church and join a Pentecostal church or keep quiet about their experience. What began to happen at midcentury was different. Ministers and laypeople from historic Christian churches began receiving the Pentecostal experience, but they chose to remain within their own denominations.

Over the next few decades, virtually every major denomination in America was affected by the Charismatic Renewal Movement. Pentecostalism began showing up in the most unexpected places, including mainline Christian churches and Ivy League campuses. Speaking in tongues and the manifestation of spiritual gifts were taking place among affluent and well-educated Episcopalians, Lutherans, Presbyterians, Methodists, and Baptists. Pastors from virtually all denominations received the experience, but the renewal was primarily a lay movement among those who were hungry and open to God. Historic churches began to be renewed in their worship and witness. Growth and renewed vitality in many of these churches was nothing less than phenomenal.

Clark Pinnock, noted Baptist theologian, spoke for many Charismatics in observing: "It is not a new doctrine we lack. What we need is a new dynamism that will make all of our old evangelical convictions operational. . . . We need not so much to be educated as to be revitalized. It is not a doctrine of the Spirit that we need but a movement of the Spirit, pervading and filling us, setting our convictions on fire."

Most classical Pentecostals were thrilled to see what God was doing in the mainstream denominations, but there were serious concerns about matters of lifestyle and doctrinal differences. Pentecostal churches were deeply influenced by holiness doctrine and lifestyles (either from the Wesleyan or Keswick views on sanctification), and by revivalism and evangelical doctrine. Churches that were experiencing charismatic renewal did not always share these traditions.

There was another glaring exception. The distinctive doctrine of Pentecostals was their belief in the baptism in the Holy Spirit, subsequent to conversion, with the initial physical evidence of speaking with other tongues as the Spirit gives the utterance. Those who called themselves Evangelicals had no place for this doctrine in their theologies. Consequently, they rejected the view that there is a reception or baptism in the Holy Spirit after conversion. Furthermore, most held that the operation of spiritual gifts had ceased. The Spirit now does His work, they believed, exclusively through the Word. These views basically set Evangelicals and Pentecostals apart.

Doctrinal tensions surfaced when the Charismatic Renewal took place among Evangelicals whose theology did not allow for an experience of baptism in the Spirit subsequent to regeneration. In some cases, Evangelicals were open to the Pentecostal view of subsequence, but they did not believe speaking with tongues was a necessary accompaniment to the experience. In *Baptism in the Holy Spirit*, New Testament scholar James Dunn championed the views of the Evangelical community. His argument was that baptism in the Spirit is not to be distinguished from conversion but that the gift of the Spirit is the climactic event in the process of becoming a Christian, the climax of conversion-initiation. He made no distinction between the theological emphases of Luke and Paul, viewing the gift of the Spirit as a soteriological and not an empowering gift. With regard to tongues or inspired speech, Dunn asserted that it was only one of many visible manifestations of the Spirit in Luke-Acts.

During the 1970s and 1980s, the Pentecostal rain began to fall on Roman Catholics. The precursor to the charismatic renewal movement among Catholics was the church council known as Vatican II (1962-65). Pope John XXIII called the council for the stated purpose of "opening the windows so that the church could get a breath of fresh air." What the church received was the fresh winds of Pentecost.

Vatican II opened the way for radical changes to occur in Roman Catholicism, including an openness to competing theologies, intercommunion with other Christians, and an openness to new forms of worship. Following the council, a liturgical movement drastically changed the forms of Catholic worship, and charisms began to appear in prayer and worship settings. By 1967, there were public manifestations of tongues.

The outpouring of the Holy Spirit in the Catholic church began at Duquesne University in Pittsburgh, Pennsylvania. Two professors were baptized in the Holy Spirit and spoke in tongues. Catholic students soon received the Spirit, falling prostrate on the floor, and experiencing manifestations similar to those of the early Pentecostals. The flame of Pentecost rapidly spread to Notre Dame University in South Bend, Indiana. Respected members of the theology faculty were baptized in the Holy Spirit. Prayer groups sprang up across the nation, and Pentecostalism began spreading like wildfire. Cardinal Suenens of Belgium joined the movement and was appointed by the pope to be his adviser concerning charismatic developments. By 1975, the "latter rain" had reached Rome, where an international conference on the Holy Spirit was held in a tent over the ancient catacombs. On Pentecost Monday, Cardinal Suenens conducted the first charismatic mass in Saint Peter's Cathedral.

The natural tendency among Roman Catholic theologians was to explain the unusual experiences of the Holy Spirit in terms of what was central to traditional Catholic theology. This meant that the work of the Spirit had to be connected with the Catholic understanding of the sacraments. Baptism in the Spirit is received, Catholics teach, through the sacrament of Confirmation, although it is not generally evident until later. What is latent from Baptism and Confirmation may be brought to a conscious level of experience or actualization at a later time. This "organic view" of baptism in the Spirit viewed the Pentecostal experience as an essential part of the "rites of initiation" (i.e., Baptism, Confirmation, and the Eucharist). They explain later experiences of tongues and other charismas in terms of a "release" or "actualization" of a grace already given in the rites of initiation. Sacramentalists hold that this perspective avoids the idea of "two baptisms," as well as two classes of Christians (i.e., the "Spirit-filled" and those who have not received "the baptism"). Tongues are not seen as "initial evidence," as classical Pentecostals believe, but as one of many authenticating gifts of the Spirit. Many Charismatics, however, express incompleteness until they speak in tongues and consider glossolalia integral to their Pentecostal experience.

A "third wave" of neocharismatics appeared during the 1980s and 1990s who were not related to the first wave of classical Pentecostals or the second wave of Charismatics. In the main, they consisted of Evangelicals and other Christians who were very much interested in the gifts of the Spirit, signs and wonders, and power encounters, but adamant in their rejection of labels like "Pentecostal" or "Charismatic." Many simply identify themselves as independent, postdenominational, restorationist, or neo-apostolic. They do not generally share the classical Pentecostal understanding of baptism in the Spirit, or tongues, but they do embrace the role of "signs and wonders" in the service of evangelism and church growth. The "third wavers" strongly encourage vibrant and expressive worship in their churches. This movement constitutes a new and strong revitalizing force that claims more adherents than the first two waves of the Pentecostal/Charismatic Movement. The most outspoken leaders of this movement have been church-growth specialist Peter Wagner and John Wimber, founder of the Vineyard movement.

During the last few decades of the twentieth century, the Pentecostal and Charismatic message has been effectively spread around the world through the means of modern technology. Televangelists Jim and Tammy Bakker, Jimmy Swaggart, Pat Robertson, and Oral Roberts understood how to use the mass media with great effectiveness. Oral Roberts and Pat Robertson, whose media ministries gained national notoriety, founded major universities: Oral Roberts University in Tulsa, Oklahoma, and Regent University in Virginia. The phenomenon of fast-growing megachurches has been a Pentecostal hallmark as well. Many of the largest churches in the world are Pentecostal and Charismatic churches.

From the days of healing evangelists like Tommy Hicks, Oral Roberts, William Branham, Kathryn Kuhlman, and T. L. Osborne, Pentecostals have held mass evangelistic crusades around the world. In recent years, Reinhard Bonnke and Benny Hinn have attracted millions through evangelistic and healing crusades in Africa, India, and other parts of the world. Protracted revivals in Toronto, Canada, and Pensacola, Florida, possessed the Pentecostal fervor and intensity of Azusa Street. Youth With a Mission (YWAM) has directed missions and humanitarian activities throughout the world. Trinity Broadcasting Network, Jimmy Swaggart's Radio and Television Ministries, and Day Star Television daily broadcast the message of Christ and Pentecost around the world.

These, and other ministries too numerous to mention, indicate that the ministry of the Holy Spirit is not finished. As Joel prophesied, God has poured out the Holy Spirit on "all flesh" for the last-days ministry of the Christian church. The wind of the Spirit blows where He will. The result has been the transformation and renewal of everything in the Spirit's path. Some streams of the movement have peaked; others have declined, but many are growing more rapidly than ever. Everywhere one looks, new ministries of the Spirit are appearing to gather the harvest and prepare the church for the soon return of Jesus Christ.

God With *Us and* In *Us*

LIFE APPLICATION

In the same year the Holy Spirit fell in Chile, a remarkable event occurred in the United States that was to be fateful for Latin America's largest nation. In South Bend, Indiana, two Swedish immigrants to the United States, Daniel Berg and Gunnar Vingren, were in attendance in a small Pentecostal prayer meeting with a few Spirit-filled friends. During the service, a prophecy was given in which the two men were directed to journey as missionaries to somewhere in the world called *Pará*.

Since no one in the room knew of any such place, the two Swedes later went to the Chicago Public Library and searched through a global atlas looking for the location of Para. After much research, they found that a province in northeastern Brazil bore that name.

Another prophecy told Berg and Vingren to go to New York City and wait for an unknown man to meet them in a certain location in the city. The man, whom they had never met nor seen before, miraculously appeared and gave them the exact amount of money to buy two one-way tickets to Brazil on a tramp steamer. They departed in 1910 and arrived in Belém, Pará, without support of any church or mission board.

At first, they attended a small Baptist church while they learned Portuguese. In a short time, the Holy Spirit began to manifest the gifts of tongues and healing in the services through Berg and Vingren. This was so unusual for the Baptist congregation that the pastor asked them to meet with their friends in the basement of the church for their Pentecostal prayer meetings. Soon, however, everyone was in the basement instead of the sanctuary. After some "serious tension," Berg and Vingren organized the first Pentecostal congregation in Brazil with eighteen members. They called their church the "Assembly of God" (this was four years before the American Assemblies of God were organized). The growth of the Brazilian Pentecostals has been nothing less than phenomenal. The Assemblies of God is now the largest Protestant denomination in all of Latin America (according to Vinson Synan *In the Latter Days*).

DISCUSSION

The Origins of Pentecostalism
1. Why, in your view, did the "latter rain" not occur before it did?
2. What were the historical and doctrinal roots of the Pentecostal Movement?

Azusa Street and Beyond
1. Describe your thoughts about the Azusa Street Revival. Would you like to be a part of this kind of revival today?

2. What were some major influences on this revival?

The Forming of Pentecostal Denominations and Missionary Fervor
1. Explain how the Azusa Street Revival gave rise to Pentecostal churches and the spreading of Pentecost around the world.
2. How are "Oneness" Pentecostals doctrinally different from other Pentecostals?
3. Give some examples of how Pentecost spread to Europe and to Latin America.

The Charismatic Renewal and the Third Wavers
1. Identify major influences on the Protestant and Catholic charismatic renewal movements.
2. Describe the attitudes of many traditional Pentecostals toward what was happening in the Charismatic Movement.
3. Doctrinally speaking, how do classical Pentecostals, Evangelicals, and Catholics differ with regard to the baptism in the Holy Spirit and evidential tongues?
4. What is different about those who are a part of the "third wave" of Pentecost?

GLOSSARY OF TERMS/CONCEPTS

Charismatic Renewal Movement: This term was being used since 1980 to describe those in the renewal movements, distinct from the classical Pentecostals, who stayed in their churches to bring revival and renewal.

Constantine (d. 337): The first Roman emperor to convert to Christianity. As the champion of Christianity, Constantine sought to unite the church. He made the bishops more prominent in the West. That encouraged the ascendancy of the Papacy and the institutionalization of the Roman church.

Finished-Work Doctrine: The Keswick emphasis on gradual, progressive sanctification, as distinct from the Wesleyan-Holiness emphasis on sanctification as a second definite work of grace that eradicates, or "puts to death," the sin nature.

Jansenism: A movement in France during the seventeenth century. The "French Prophets" manifested various charisms, including prophecy and tongues.

Montanism: A second-century apocalyptic movement that emphasized the imminent return of Christ and a strict morality for the faithful. The leaders of the movement did not intend their prophecies and ecstasies to undermine the authority of Scripture. Nonetheless, the emerging church authorities considered Montanus and his followers heretical.

Sacramentalists: Those in Catholic and Protestant churches who place high value on the sacraments as the means God uses to confirm divine promises to believers and bring the recipients of grace into the truths they represent. Sacramentalists generally stress participation in the sacraments more than inner transformation (e.g., conversion) and personal piety.

Third Wave: Mainline Evangelicals who believe in "signs and wonders" but disdain labels like "Pentecostal" or "Charismatic." This movement originated at Fuller Theological Seminary in the early 1980s under the teaching of John Wimber and Peter Wagner. This movement is believed to be the largest of the three waves of the Holy Spirit in the twentieth century.

RESOURCES FOR ADDITIONAL STUDY

Blumhofer, Edith L., Russell P. Spittler, and Grant A. Wacker. *Pentecostal Currents in American Protestantism*. Chicago: U of Illinois P, 1999.

Burgess, Stanley M., ed., and Eduard van der Maas, assoc. ed. *New International Dictionary of Pentecostal and Charismatic Movements*. Grand Rapids: Zondervan, 2001.

Cox, Harvey. *Fire From Heaven: The Rise of Pentecostal Spirituality in the Twenty-First Century*. New York: Addison-Wesley, 1994.

Goff, James R., and Grant Wacker, eds. *Portraits of a Generation: Early Pentecostal Leaders*. Fayetteville, Ark.: U of Arkansas P, 2001.

Hollenweger, Walter. *Pentecostalism: Origins and Developments Worldwide*. Peabody, Mass.: Hendrickson, 1997.

McDonnell, Kilian. *Charismatic Renewal and the Churches*. New York: Seabury, 1976.

McDonnell, Kilian, and George Montague. *Christian Initiation and Baptism in the Holy Spirit: Evidence From the First Eight Centuries*. Collegeville, Minn.: Liturgical, 1991.

Synan, Vinson. *The Century of the Holy Spirit*. Nashville: Nelson, 2001.

Lesson 10

Our Pentecostal Identity

Church historian David Steinmetz observed in *Theology Today* that "people who have lost their memories no longer remember who they are . . . they can no longer function effectively in the present and have no secure plans for the future. We must have contact with the past," Steinmetz noted, "for the sake of the present and the future." Steinmetz's point is that the identity of a church is as important as one's individual identity.

If Pentecostals are to function effectively in the present and move confidently into their future, it is imperative that they have a clear understanding of who they are and what God has called them to be. Contemporary Pentecostals must rediscover the power of those convictions that shaped their life and character, gave passion and vitality to their movement, and equipped them for witness and service as a "last days" church. Our task in this lesson is to reflect on who we are as classical Pentecostals and what we have been called to be at this time in our history. To that end, we will focus on (1) what it means to be a Pentecostal Christian, (2) doctrine and spirituality, and (3) contemporary issues and challenges.

I. WHAT IT MEANS TO BE A PENTECOSTAL CHRISTIAN

When the phenomenon of Pentecost occurred in the apostolic church, there was little understanding of what was happening. There was misunderstanding then, as there has been in our time, concerning the work of the Holy Spirit. The question on everyone's mind seemed to be, "What does this mean?" (Acts 2:12).

John Wesley faced a similar situation in the eighteenth century when many in England were confused about the rise of a new movement called *Methodism*. They could only regard the movement as some new form of piety with strange behaviors and a different doctrine. Wesley was concerned that Methodism was being identified with these erroneous notions instead of true Christian faith. To clear up some of the confusion, he wrote a tract called "The Character of a Methodist," in which he turned his attention to the distinguishing marks of a true Methodist.

In a similar way, it is necessary today to reflect on and restate what it means to be a true Pentecostal Christian. For Christians living in the spiritual and charismatic ethos of our time, this is a critical issue.

Pentecost cannot be rightly separated from Jesus Christ. The Spirit's relationship to Christ is central. The New Testament places no focus on the Spirit apart from Him (Rom. 8:9). In John 7:39, the apostle says, "As yet there was no Spirit because Jesus had not yet been glorified" (Moffatt). John was not saying the Holy Spirit did not exist before this time. We know the Holy Spirit is the eternal Spirit who participated in the creation of the world (Gen. 1:2) and was active throughout the history of Israel. John was saying the Holy Spirit would not be fully released until the work of Jesus Christ made Him available to the Church. The resurrection and glorification of Christ made the Spirit's power and presence available.

Pentecost brought to the church an unprecedented outpouring of the Holy Spirit to equip it for the mission that centered in the risen Lord. The Spirit did not mean something different from Jesus. It meant that those who received the Spirit could belong to Jesus in a special way, as those who had been breathed upon by the risen Christ (John 20:21-22).

In the Spirit, God makes His claim on our whole person for the realization of His full purpose for our lives. That claim is filled with meaning and power through the fullness of the Spirit's work in us. Through the Holy Spirit, we are birthed into Christ and bear the fruit of His indwelling presence. Through the Spirit, we come to our identity in Christ. The Spirit empowers a sanctified and holy life in Christ. The Holy Spirit is the power and source of spiritual gifting that glorifies Christ and edifies the church. The Spirit bears witness to Christ through His power and presence in our lives.

Baptism in the Holy Spirit was never meant to be an add-on experience that would serve as the basis for a new tradition or denominational distinctive. The New Testament expectation is that all who are in Christ should experience the fullness of the Spirit in their lives. Pentecost was not a divine suggestion. Jesus commanded His disciples to remain in Jerusalem until they had been filled with the Holy Spirit (Luke 24:49). The early church maintained the expectation that all Christians should be filled with the Spirit, and that expectation should continue to be emphasized today.

As eschatological gift, the Holy Spirit constitutes the continuing presence of the kingdom of God in the life of believers. Living under the reign of God demands repentance and a repudiation of the old life. Those who participate in the life of the Kingdom must be committed to truthfulness, the pursuit of holiness, and a life of love.

God works through various stages of a believer's life to transform his or her character and bring loving obedience to the will of God. There is no need to argue, as so many have, about the question of sanctification as a progressive or instantaneous work. The core issue is that the essence of a sanctified life is a love that obeys Christ, transformed and complete in its effect. It begins in regeneration and admits to a continual increase, so long as one lives in an unbroken relationship with Christ. As Pentecostal theologian R. Hollis Gause notes, "The believer, from the first moment of his faith in Christ, is living in the Spirit. To be saved and live a godly life is to live in and by the agency of the Holy Spirit."

Classical Pentecostals are committed to a baptism in the Holy Spirit that is subsequent to conversion. That experience, however, must not be separated from the unification of life in the Spirit to which the Scriptures attest. What baptism in the Spirit brings into the lives of believers is empowerment for prophetic witness. Baptism in the Spirit essentially represents a release of an already indwelling Spirit for the purpose of greater power and effectiveness in Christian witness and service. There is, so to speak, the "inhale" of the Spirit that draws us out of the world and into the life of the Spirit. Through the "exhale" of the Spirit, we are sent back into the world, empowered vocationally and charismatically, for participation in the mission of the Holy Spirit.

II. DOCTRINE AND SPIRITUALITY

In 1958, liberal theologian Henry Van Dusen wrote an article for *Life* magazine in which he described the rapidly rising Pentecostal Movement as "the third force in Christendom." The phrase caught on, and it soon became common to call the movement the "third force," and to place Pentecostals alongside Roman Catholics and Protestants as the leading traditions in Christendom.

The "third force" designation was meant to be a compliment to the growth and vitality of the Pentecostal/Charismatic Movement. It emphasized the spiritual benefits that large numbers of people were experiencing because of the movement's spirituality and doctrine. While Pentecostals felt gratified that other Christians had finally begun to recognize the viability and vitality of their movement, there was something about the "third force" designation that made them uncomfortable. Pentecostals did not think of themselves as an alternative form of Christianity—as a "new force" in Christendom—but as a latter-day continuation of the work of the Holy Spirit that early Christians knew and experienced in the New Testament. The heritage Pentecostals have always claimed is one that defines its center in Jesus Christ and the fulfillment of His mission in the world through the presence and power of the Holy Spirit.

Pentecostals believe and proclaim a full-gospel message of salvation, sanctification, healing, spiritual gifts, baptism in the Holy Spirit with the evidence of speaking in tongues as the Spirit gives the utterance, and the premillennial second coming of Jesus Christ. They embrace the ecumenical Christian creeds, believe in God as Creator and Preserver of the world, and insist on the full inspiration and authority of God's Word. Most Pentecostals are Arminian in doctrine and are passionate about the evangelization of the world. They are firmly rooted in the Reformation doctrines of justification by faith, the priesthood of all believers, a biblical understanding of church and sacraments, and obedience to the life pattern of Jesus Christ.

Spirituality, for Pentecostals, is not a buzzword or mystical experience. It is not a technique or feel-good experience a person can have, apart from a Christian commitment in every dimension of one's life. This includes, among other things, the spiritual disciplines of prayer, Bible reading, loving obedience to God's Word, and a Christian lifestyle. True spirituality is a way of life, an informed and heartfelt engagement in Christian worship, and growth and maturity in Christ. True Christian experience and spirituality, Pentecostals believe, must have the Christ-character of Jesus (that is, the presence of the Spirit in Jesus) as their norm. All forms of spirituality and piety that do not conform to the Christ model are, in one way or another, in error and distorted.

The character of Pentecostal spirituality was beautifully modeled in the early Christian community. Scripture describes these Spirit-filled believers:

> They devoted themselves to the apostles' teaching and to the fellowship, to the breaking of bread and to prayer. Everyone was filled with awe, and many wonders and miraculous signs were done by the apostles. All the

believers were together and had everything in common. Selling their possessions and goods, they gave to anyone as he had need. Every day they continued to meet together in the temple courts. They broke bread in their homes and ate together with glad and sincere hearts, praising God and enjoying the favor of all the people. And the Lord added to their number daily those who were being saved (Acts 2:42-47).

It is significant that the first mark of the Spirit-filled church mentioned in this passage is study. The early Christians eagerly devoted themselves to the apostles' teaching. The apostolic church was a learning and studying church. The Holy Spirit had opened a school in Jerusalem and the apostles were the appointed teachers. Early Christians did not disdain doctrine, nor did they suppose that instruction was unnecessary. They knew Jesus had authorized the apostles to be the teachers of the church, so they submitted to their authority. True spirituality does not allow for the dichotomizing of the head from the heart. We are to love God with our minds as well as our emotions. Spirit-filled Christians should always approach learning and study as an act of worship, bowing the mind before the Author of all truth.

A second mark of spiritual worship in the apostolic church was their unity in the Spirit, their togetherness and fellowship. The unity of the early church was more than mere friendship and camaraderie; it was the fellowship of the Holy Spirit—the kind of unity and fellowship that binds believers together under the lordship of Jesus Christ (*koinonia*). True Pentecostal worship provides a spiritual environment for fellowship, comfort, exhortation, and prayer for one another. The "fellowship of the saints" in worship settings provides strength, courage, and edification for believers. When the church hears the Word of God, it is reminded of God's faithfulness to His promises. When it drinks from the cup and breaks the bread, it remembers the continuity of His grace.

Worship is the life of the church. Through its worship, the church witnesses to the resurrected Christ who lives in His church through the Holy Spirit. Pentecostal worship is joyous and alive. Pentecostals are widely known for anointed and spirited singing. Songs of worship should reflect both the freedom of the Spirit (e.g., praise and worship choruses) and the faithful continuity of God's grace in the church (e.g., hymns).

Pentecostal spirituality provides for a free-flowing operation of the *charismata* (spiritual gifts) and for "signs and wonders" as God wills. The gifts can never be rightly separated from the Giver, Jesus Christ (Eph. 4:7-13). In giving the Holy Spirit, Christ has given to His church all that is necessary for its life and mission. The Holy Spirit operates in believers to witness to and glorify Jesus Christ. When Christ is exalted, the church is edified.

A charismatic community always stands in need of organization and structure as well as freedom. The early church was not a free-floating enterprise, operating without order or structure. As the *Logos* took on human form in Jesus Christ, the church needs structural form through which Christ's work can be extended to the world. The "spiritual church" and "organized church" always need each other. They cannot rightly be separated, but neither should they be confused. The former provides the agenda, the vision, and inspiration for the work of the church. The latter provides the vehicle through which the purpose and ideal of the spiritual church finds expression. It is the former that keeps the latter renewed so that it can, through the living Christ, maintain its vision and fulfill its purpose.

Above all else, a truly Pentecostal community is a Christian community. This means it must be a loving and serving community. The Holy Spirit does not close up believers in themselves but opens them up toward others. Love is more than emotion and sentimentality; love manifests itself in self-giving action. Love feeds the hungry, clothes the naked, befriends the friendless, and sets the captives free. Love is meant to be enfleshed in our actions, and in us, as it was in Jesus. Compassion for others is a vital part of the Pentecostal heritage, as it was in the early church. Through care for the sick, the poor, the orphaned, unwed mothers, drug addicts and alcoholics, as well as those dispossessed by natural disasters, the church testifies of its love and service.

The first Pentecost accelerated the spirit of inclusiveness in the early church as the Holy Spirit began to break down social, economic, ethnic, and cultural barriers that hindered the gospel. The Jews had long-standing prejudices against Samaritans in particular and Gentiles in general. But the work of the Spirit in the church served to build bridges rather than barriers to these people as the Spirit was poured out on "all flesh."

Pentecostals today are still learning the importance of inclusiveness regarding gender and race, but the movement has generally identified with all races, the poor, and the disinherited around the world. It has historically reached out to those on the fringes of society. In Latin America, Africa, Indonesia, and Third World countries around the world, Pentecostal churches have enjoyed phenomenal growth because they identify with all the people and work among the poor. Pentecostal churches today are enjoying the fruits of this inclusiveness.

III. ISSUES AND CHALLENGES

Living as Pentecostal Christians in a postmodern and post-Christian world is challenging. The spirit of our time challenges our courage and resolve to be the kind of people God has called us to be. Our greatest challenge is to stay connected with the solid substance of biblical truth and the tradition that has shaped who we are. This requires more than understanding; it requires the spiritual courage to be what we have been called to be in the power of the Holy Spirit.

Some challenges relate to living on the extremes and boundaries of true Pentecostal experience. There are those who have "settled down" in their experience, who tend to identify "Spirit-filled" and "Spirit-led" terminology with ecstatic and emotional extremism. This spiritual paranoia restricts them to "measured" and cognitive considerations of what to expect from the work of the Holy Spirit. Another extreme, alluded to by Hollis Gause, is more emotional and pragmatic in nature. Gause describes this approach to life in the Spirit as one that confirms whatever one is, or whatever one is doing, when he or she is being "blessed." This shallow form of emotional pragmatism is then passed off as the approval and guidance of the Holy Spirit.

A true Pentecost requires both sound doctrine and an authentic experience. It will not do to emphasize one at the expense of the other. On the one hand, the Spirit's work cannot be relegated to what is "safe" and "conventional." The Holy Spirit is sovereign and full of surprises. He blows where He will. On the other hand, the ministry of the Holy Spirit cannot be relegated in the extreme to the realm of emotion, experience, and signs and wonders. The emergence of Pentecostal churches and the Charismatic Movement brought some ambiguities and unbalanced views regarding the work of the Holy Spirit. Among these is a strong focus on the experience of the Spirit, but little emphasis on the purpose of the Holy Spirit. Another is emphasis on the doctrine and purpose of the Holy Spirit, while neglecting the power of the Spirit. Just as a pair of scissors cannot function properly without both blades, the church must know both the power and the purpose of the Holy Spirit.

Pentecostals must seek a full-orbed pneumatology, but above all else they must take seriously the fact that the Spirit's primary work is to reveal and develop the character of Christ in the believer. Purity and power cannot be rightly separated in the Christian life. Other issues must not be elevated above their intended purpose. Pentecostals, for example, rightly believe there is glossolalic evidence of the Spirit's fullness in the life of the believer. However, this should not lead to the kind of glossocentrism that confuses many with regard to the real purpose of Pentecost. Signs of the Spirit should not be confused with the purpose of the Spirit.

The size, strength, and acceptance of the Pentecostal Movement have increased significantly. In many parts of the world today, Pentecostals and their constituents comprise high percentages of the population, and their social, economic, and political influence is no longer negligible. More is now expected of Pentecostals than when the movement was small and struggling. Determining the kind of spiritual and moral leadership the Pentecostal church can and should provide as a major movement is an important consideration. It should not be left to chance. I suggest three areas that need attention.

The first has to do with handling the Scriptures. Pentecostals have always held to the authority of the Bible in all matters relating to faith and practice. The church must not move away from the Bible as the measure of all claims to truth. But "holding to the authority of the Bible" will not mean very much if we fail to take it in its wholeness or interpret it loosely.

A partial pneumatological perspective or experience will obviously lack the holistic perspective of one drawn from a complete Christian theology. A selective and narrow approach to Scripture that oversimplifies complex issues, ignores a holistic understanding of the Bible, and sacrifices Christian doctrine to existential experience will prove fatal. In our postmodern setting, Pentecostals must appreciate the truth and meaning of Bible texts. They need a better understanding of how to read and interpret these texts and reflect theologically on their meaning. One of the great needs of Pentecostal parishioners is for more and better expository preaching, so the meaning and purpose of Scripture texts can be carefully explained from the pulpit. To these ends, Pentecostal churches must make a commitment of will and resources to theological training and discipleship formation.

Second, Pentecostals must not ignore their responsibility to develop Christian character. Character may begin with an experience, but a crisis experience does not produce a Christian heart and mind. Christian formation and moral development is of necessity a process that requires training, mentoring, and good models. It is not enough for the church to emphasize a crisis experience followed by a commitment to "keep the rules." The importance of emphasizing right and godly decisions can never be minimized, but what is needed is "trained habit"—a disposition to do what is right that has been formed through one's thought life, spiritual condition, and disciplined habits. Like a garden that requires both the resources of nature and the hard disciplined work of the gardener, virtuous and godly living require the kind of trained habit that only God can produce in us, but that we must be willing to practice and nurture.

Third, the pull of social and cultural accommodation is very tempting to Pentecostals. A movement seeking social acceptance and intellectual credibility must carefully guard against accommodation to the world, even in its more subtle forms. It is easy to compromise the integrity of one's convictions and behavior without being fully conscious that one has done so. In the pragmatic environment of America, the "success ethic" has driven much of the Pentecostal compromise with worldly values and lifestyles.

If there was too much "hardness" and "legalism" in the early days of the movement, it could be argued that the Achilles heel of the movement in more recent times has been the sanctification of success. This accommodation to culture is manifested in those who willingly substitute style for substance, who glorify the "glitz" of the media, and put forward celebrity preachers and musicians in the interest of growth and success. It is seen in those who measure the effectiveness of Kingdom work in terms of numbers, finances, buildings, and programs. Failure to discern this accommodation for what it is, and the lack of will to address it, will put blight on Pentecostal integrity. Pentecostals can profit from serious reflection and soul-searching in this area of their common life.

At this point in our history, it is important to consider our future as well as our past. If the church is to be a community of character, engaging the world in the name of Christ, it must reject any tendency to settle into religious narcissism. A church called to "live in the Spirit" must, by reason of its own character and mission, be one that is morally sensitive, cares deeply about human need, and commits itself to the purposes of God. And, it must do so according to the model of Jesus Christ. Involvement for involvement's sake must not dictate the life and work of the church. Pentecostal Christians, like all others who have been effective instruments of God throughout Christian history, must be a discerning people—knowing when, where, and how God is at work in His world.

LIFE APPLICATION

A friend of mine returned from China a few years ago, after the Cultural Revolution, and told me about some of his experiences there. One of the problems the people are having, he said, is identity. During the Cultural Revolution, the Communist authorities tried to rid the people of their past. In an effort to turn the country in a new direction, they tried to destroy everything about the past they believed would hinder the success of the new revolution. They destroyed books, museums, and killed off the intelligentsia in hopes this would eradicate all links with their past way of life. The result is that the present generation hardly knows who they are. Consequently, they are finding it difficult to function in the present or plan for any kind of meaningful future.

We have all witnessed victims of Alzheimer's who have lost contact with their past. The effect of this terrible malady is not simply loss of contact with the past but with the present and future as well. It renders one ineffective and meaningless. The same thing can happen to a church that has spiritual Alzheimer's. Churches need to stay in contact with their roots. Our Pentecostal heritage is important to us, because it helps us understand who we are and what God has called us to be in these last days. While it is important to have a rich spiritual heritage we can appreciate and draw inspiration from, it is equally important that we not live in the past or in anxiety about an uncertain future. The Holy Spirit is the eternal Spirit. He indwells us now and will be our sufficiency in the future that God has in store for us.

DISCUSSION

What It Means to Be a Pentecostal Christian
1. Why is the work of the Holy Spirit inseparable from Christ? Give some explanation.
2. Do you think most Christians understand that they are to be "filled with the Spirit"? Give the reason for your answer.

Doctrine and Spirituality
1. Is Pentecostal doctrine, in your view, biblically sound? Why is this your view?
2. Describe or explain what Pentecostal spirituality means to you.

Issues and Challenges
1. What do you foresee as the future of the Pentecostal Movement?
2. What, in your opinion, is the greatest challenge facing contemporary Pentecostals?

GLOSSARY OF TERMS/CONCEPTS

Arminianism: A system of theology founded on the thought of James Arminius (1560-1609), a Dutch theologian and pastor. Arminius taught that predestination or election is based on God's foreknowledge of whether or not an individual freely accepts or rejects Christ. This view was in contrast to that of John Calvin and Martin Luther, who held that predestination is an unconditional action of God.

Ecumenical Creeds: Four major creedal statements in the early church are generally regarded as authoritative in both Catholic and Protestant churches: (1) the Apostles' Creed; (2) the Nicene Creed; (3) the Chalcedonian Definition; (4) the Athanasian Creed.

Expository Preaching: A form of preaching that seeks to understand and proclaim what a text means and communicates on its own.

Koinonia: A Greek word meaning "fellowship," "communion," or "sharing together." It refers to Christian believers sharing together the life of Christ through the Holy Spirit.

Sacraments: The two sacraments (ordinances) accepted and practiced by virtually all classical Pentecostals are water baptism and the Lord's Supper (Holy Communion).

Spirituality: From a Pentecostal perspective, spirituality is centered in one's relationship with God and life in the Spirit. True spirituality must be Christ-centered and Bible-based.

RESOURCES FOR ADDITIONAL STUDY

Land, Steven J. *Pentecostal Spirituality: A Passion for the Kingdom*. Sheffield, England: Sheffield Academic Press, 1993.

Macchia, Frank D. *Baptized in the Spirit: A Global Pentecostal Theology*. Grand Rapids: Zondervan, 2006.

Sims, John A. *Our Pentecostal Heritage*. Cleveland, Tenn.: Pathway, 1995.

Synan, Vinson. *The Century of the Holy Spirit*. Nashville, Tenn.: Nelson, 2001.